CHINA:

NEW AGE AND NEW OUTLOOK

A DA CAPO PRESS REPRINT SERIES

China

in the 20th century

CHINA:
NEW AGE AND
NEW OUTLOOK

by PING-CHIA KUO

DA CAPO PRESS • NEW YORK • 1975

Library of Congress Cataloging in Publication Data

Kuo, Pin-chia.
  China, new age and new outlook.

  (China in the 20th century)
  Reprint of the 1956 ed. published by Knopf, New York.
  Includes index.
  1. China—Politics and government—1949-
  2. China—Foreign relations—1949-   3. China—
  Economic policy. I. Title.
  DS777.55.K75 1975   320.9'51'05   74-30079
  ISBN 0-306-70679-2

This Da Capo Press edition of *China: New Age and New Outlook*
is an unabridged republication of the first edition published
in New York in 1956. It is reprinted with the permission of
Alfred A. Knopf, Inc.

Published by Da Capo Press, Inc.
A Subsidiary of Plenum Publishing Corporation
227 West 17th Street, New York, N.Y. 10011

Manufactured in the United States of America

CHINA:

NEW AGE AND NEW OUTLOOK

CHINA:

NEW AGE

AND

NEW OUTLOOK

PING-CHIA KUO

ALFRED A. KNOPF

NEW YORK 1956

L.C. catalog card number: 56–5605

© Ping-chia Kuo, 1956

THIS IS A BORZOI BOOK,
PUBLISHED BY ALFRED A. KNOPF, INC.

FIRST EDITION

TO MY WIFE

ANNE

PREFACE

✿

In the present book, I have endeavored to discuss the great changes going on in China as an integral phase in the evolution of her people. Many writers, viewing the current scene from without rather than from within, speak in such terms as the "loss of China to Communism." Such an approach does not probe deeply enough into the reasons for the success of Communism in China; it appears to stem from an unconsidered premise that regards the ferment in China as incidental to the foreign policies of the Western nations. This book makes a different approach to the subject. It seeks to appraise and interpret the current developments as a stage in the broad sweep of Chinese history, to search out the fundamental trends that have led to the triumph of Communism, and to discuss the major problems involved in this process.

When viewed in this perspective, certain aspects of Communist rule that form the usual subjects of contemporary writings become important only as symptoms, while deeper historical trends, often forgotten amidst the crises and passions of the day, and yet of lasting significance in explaining the march of men and events, take on a new prominence. I am convinced that the affairs of China cannot

really be understood unless one has a "feel" for the country
and its people and under its promptings proceeds to view
events as millions of Chinese would see them. I have therefore not contented myself with the mere collation of facts,
but have sought to recapture and reveal the spirit of the
changing China.

The present study is not confined to the period of Communist rule. It is not even confined to the last two or three
decades. It is essentially a broad look at a new age in China,
taking in pertinent points in China's great past as well as
whatever can be adjudged of her future. Although I have
had to be concise and selective, I have tried to evolve a perspective based on what may be considered the vital forces
in Chinese history. I have also avoided pedantic analysis
and partisan controversy. For instance, an overemphasis on
the discrepancies between Mao Tse-tung's revolutionary
doctrine and Marxism-Leninism to the neglect of the Chinese genesis and background of Mao's revolutionary career
is as unhelpful as it is inadvisable. At the same time, I have
worked from a conviction that the Communist record is
neither all good nor all evil, and that inasmuch as the new
regime is an accomplished fact, it is essential that we know
its strong points as well as its weaknesses. Accordingly, I
have judged wherever judgment seemed useful. My readers will find plenty of praise and blame in these pages;
they are not, however, such as partisan interests might dictate, but only as realism or objectivity would demand.

Throughout the ages, historians in China have debated
whether new heroes create a new age (*"yin hsiung tsao
shih shih"*) or a new age creates new heroes (*"shih shih
tsao yin hsiung"*). The dramatic developments dealt with
in this volume bear out the fact that both processes have

been at work. Without the economic and social forces making for revolution, plus the impact of eight years of war with Japan, it is doubtful whether the Communists would have risen to total power. Now that they have control, however, the leaders in Peking are molding the coming age with their ambitious programs for internal reconstruction and for a new order in the Far East. The interaction of an extraordinary age and extraordinary men accounts for the heightened pace of events that are unfolding before our eyes. The Chinese Revolution was born only forty-five years ago, on the eve of World War I. The Communist Party was not founded and the Kuomintang not reorganized until thirty years ago, at the time of Presidents Harding and Coolidge and the first Soviet Five-Year Plan. Yet beginning with the Sian and Lukouchiao incidents, in the years of the New Deal in America and Hitler's rise to power in Europe, China has moved ahead to the position of a great world power in less than two decades. So rapid a rebirth of an ancient and great nation cannot but have the most far-reaching influence both on the Chinese people and on the rest of the world. This book attempts to convey some of the import of this great ferment.

As Ku Yen-wu said, *"T'ien hsia hsing wang, p'i fu yu tse"* ("Everybody has a share of responsibility in the rise and fall of his country"). It is in the spirit of this great scholar that I have undertaken to write this volume. If it succeeds in stirring a creative interest in China and in quickening a sense of appreciation of the great issues at stake, my effort will be amply rewarded.

In preparing this volume, I have had the encouragement and wise counsel of my wife, whose deep love for China has given her a sensitive understanding of the Chinese charac-

ter and history. I am deeply indebted to her for discussing
the text with me as well as for corrections in my writing.

P. C. K.

Palm Acres
Sebastopol, California
October 1955

CONTENTS

I. *The Process of an Economic and Social Revolution*   3

II. *The Foundations of Communist Strength and Success*   47

III. *The Character and Mood of the New Regime*   81

IV. *The Drive for Great-Power Status*   118

V. *The Problems of Reconstruction*   166

VI. *The Outlook: Peace or War?*   201

INDEX   *follows page* 231

CHINA:

NEW AGE AND NEW OUTLOOK

I

THE PROCESS OF AN ECONOMIC
AND SOCIAL REVOLUTION

✿

THERE is a famous saying in China that in approaching the
Twenty-four Dynastic Histories, one does not know where
to begin. The study of Chinese history would indeed be
an interminable task if one tried to exhaust the details of
kings and dynasties, wars and invasions, or the doings of
ministers, governors, and generals. Fortunately, however,
these details do not represent the decisive influences that
mark the development of the Chinese people. The course
of history in China, as indeed in any other country, is
actually determined by the powerful economic and social
forces that affect the fortunes of the people as a whole.
Despite the vicissitudes of forty centuries, the evolution of
Chinese society and economy, particularly of the problems
and needs of the masses, forms a continuous thread of
change, which alone can explain the events of our time.

It is in the light of this process of economic and social
revolution that the current upheaval may be assessed in
proper perspective. The rise of the Communists to power
is no isolated event. Certainly it is not merely the work of
a group of revolutionary extremists. Its roots reach far
back into the structure of the old society, the abuses of

government, the inequalities and miseries suffered by the people, and a widespread demand for change.

From 200 B.C. until World War II, Chinese society was composed of two segments: a vast peasantry embracing over eighty per cent of the population, and a small minority made up of privileged groups. The peasantry was the only productive sector. The privileged groups were nonproductive. Under such a social structure, as long as the numerically small privileged groups lived off the production of the peasants without throttling their livelihood, there were peace and a measure of well-being. That, indeed, was the situation in ancient times under the feudal system of the Chou dynasty. In that age, though the peasants worked the land for the nobles, land was feudal grant rather than private property, and was equally distributed among the peasants under the so-called *"Ching T'ien"* system (literally "well field," meaning equal plots). As land was not for sale, there was no concentration of ownership in private hands, and consequently there was no landlord class. From the Ch'in and Han dynasties onward (roughly from 200 B.C.), however, the situation changed completely. With the collapse of the feudal system, the hereditary nobility gave way to new classes of power and wealth. Land was freely bought and sold. This led inevitably to the concentration of land in the hands of the new privileged groups, and to the growing importance of landlords as a social class. The far-reaching influences of such a change governed the development of Chinese society and economy for approximately the next two thousand years. A great proportion of the peasantry continued to till the land, but did not own it, while the small and nonproductive sector of privileged groups owned the land and exploited the labor of the peasantry. This is the basic picture of traditional Chinese society, in which the roots of the Revolution are to be found.

In the course of these twenty centuries the line of demarcation between the two segments of Chinese society became more sharply drawn. The privileged groups that operated the government came increasingly under the influence of the landlord class. As a rule, whenever a new dynasty was founded, the top social crust consisted of the monarchy, the imperial princes, and the military men who helped establish the new regime. But for two reasons these groups could not run the government without the help of the landlord class. Economically, the landlords virtually controlled the tens of thousands of villages. The government had therefore to depend upon them as tax-collectors for its revenues. Administratively, too, the landlord class was the only group with the leisure to study and to master politics. Thus, the government had to fall back on them for the necessary personnel (the scholar-literati) to operate the administrative machinery. This is why in every dynasty the Chinese government was virtually run by men who came from landowning families.

This tight grip on power by the landlord class was made more enduring by the adoption of Confucianism as the standard education for all officials. Anyone who followed a different school of thought was disqualified for government office. Confucian teachings no doubt stressed high ethical values and imbued men with substantial personal qualities so that scholars in government were a source of strength when compared, for instance, with military men. But it is quite clear that by upholding authoritarianism and conformity to the established order, Confucianism as a state cult was calculated to perpetuate the pre-eminence of the landlord class. For twenty centuries Confucianism blocked progress and change, taught the oppressed to obey, and impressed upon the minds of men the virtue of upholding the *status quo*.

So close an identification of the government with landlord interests could not but produce the worst of social abuses. At the beginning of a dynasty, when the alliance was first formed, the government would receive full taxes from all landowners according to the tax registers. But as the landlords fixed their hold upon the government, they managed to withdraw their own land from taxation through a variety of evasive practices. As the government could not exist without revenues, more taxes were shifted to the shoulders of the peasants. The resulting inequality of the tax burden was one of the greatest grievances of the peasants in the old society. Together with land hunger and high rent, it formed the three focal points of conflict between the two segments of Chinese society.

There was a change of dynasty roughly every three hundred years. But the basic sociological pattern remained the same; the landlord-scholar-military combination could not be broken. It controlled the wealth, held the power, and provided the skill to run the government. Above all, it was opposed to change. Even foreign conquerors could not break its grip but had to submit to it. Under this immutable scheme of things, the experience of the West, where the Industrial Revolution brought the middle class into prominence and counterbalanced the one-sided agricultural economy, was never paralleled in China's history. As there was no middle class, there was no force to fight against the domination of the privileged groups.

From the standpoint of social development, the greatest effect of the concentration of power and wealth was the development among the privileged groups of a spirit of detachment from the vast agrarian population. At all points of contact, economically, politically, and philosophically, their interests ran counter to those of the peasants. As a result, the traditional government of China was operated without the broad base of mass support. Nor did it seem that the privileged groups were at all interested in organizing, or learning to organize, the masses. On the contrary, their greatest concern was to keep the masses at a distance. The intense specialization necessary to master Confucian learning made government a monopoly of the scholar-literati. Furthermore, the family system, originally the effective basis of government in the days of ancient feudalism, was utilized by Confucian scholars to foster a mass concern for family relationships, with the result that the people became absorbed in the affairs of the clan and did not develop an active interest in government. Meanwhile, the government was maintained by sheer political and military power, which further widened the gap between the government and the people. The failure to develop a capacity for mass organization was one of the outstanding features of the *ancien régime* in China. Regardless of whether the country was strong or weak, united or torn apart, privilege rather than popular rights was the underlying spirit of the state.

With such a sociological structure, the need for an economic and social revolution became increasingly acute. Accordingly, throughout the centuries, from the Western Han (202 B.C.–A.D. 9) through each succeeding dynasty to the Ming (1368–1644) and the Ch'ing (1644–1911), the peasants frequently revolted. Among others, one may note these well-known uprisings: the Red Eyebrows at the end of the Western Han dynasty; the Yellow Turbans at the end of the Eastern Han; the Huang Ch'ao uprising at the end of the T'ang; the Fang La revolt at the end of the Sung; the rebellions led by Li Tsu-ch'eng and Chang Hsien-chung at the end of the Ming; and the Nien Fei and the Taiping in the latter part of the Ch'ing dynasty. In all these instances, the revolts were unsuccessful. For the most part, they arose out of unbearable hardships rather than as conscious or organized movements against the government. As a rule, the cause was flood or drought, followed by failure of crops and famine. This drove the desperate farmers to action, but there was neither organization nor leadership nor a systematic program. Whatever military force there was among the rebels lacked political direction. Above all, the embattled farmers were notoriously short of trained personnel to administer any territory they might bring under their control.

There were indeed a few cases, notably the founding of the Han and the Ming dynasties, where popular revolts managed to set up a new regime. But the restoration of the old sociological structure took place almost immediately as a result of the re-entry of the privileged groups into the government. The victorious military men were unable to run their government without enlisting the co-operation of the landlord-scholar class. When the new regimes were first launched, to be sure, some measures were usually adopted to lighten the burden of the people, but they were short-lived and fragmentary. Whenever peasant relief seemed effective, it was due more to the decrease in population preceding the emergence of a new dynasty than to a positive policy for social amelioration. There was no fundamental program for dealing with the abuses under landlordism.

The only bold measure, launched by Wang Mang, who usurped the power of the Western Han, was a dismal failure. This daring reformer caused a veritable holocaust when, as Emperor of the Hsin dynasty (A.D. 9–23), he ordered the nationalization of land, the abolition of slavery, the grant of agricultural credits, the stabilization of prices, and a state monopoly of trade and industry. As was to be expected, the opposition of the privileged groups was so violent that the orders for these reforms had to be quickly rescinded. Rather than pointing the way for revolutionary action, the outcome of the entire Wang Mang episode underscored the indestructible strength of the landlord-scholar-militarist combination.

Under the Northern Wei, the Sui, and the early T'ang dynasties (roughly from the fifth to the seventh centuries of our era), the *"Chün T'ien"* system was introduced. This admirable system was originally meant to give certain relief to the peasantry by a plan of equalized land allocations. Some scholars think that there is a considerable similarity between this system and the Communist land-redistribution policy. This view, however, is not warranted by facts. The *"Chün T'ien"* system did not really touch the large landlords of its time. Much of the land allocated was abandoned or waste land. Furthermore, shortly following the allocation, glaring inequalities in landownership reappeared. Inasmuch as land could be freely bought and sold, the rich soon acquired the holdings of the poor. This was to be expected because the system was launched and enforced by a government dominated by the privileged groups. It must be stressed that the primary objective of the *"Chün T'ien"* system was the resettlement of idle lands rather than land equalization for its own sake.

At any rate, from the time when Yang Yen, a prime minister of the late T'ang period, introduced the biannual tax system in 780, until the twentieth century, no further effort was made even in the direction of this type of equalization. Private ownership of land was left to develop on a laissez-faire basis. Thus despite numerous peasant revolts and certain well-intentioned measures for amelioration, there never was an economic and social revolution in the real sense. Rebels and reformers alike desired to break down the large concentrations of land, but they failed to find a solution for the two key aspects of the problem: namely, how to uproot the omnipotent influence of the landlords, and how to organize the agricultural population for effective action.

The question then arises: how did the old social structure with its glaring inequalities persist for so long a time? Here it is important to note one remarkable feature that characterized the Chinese economy for the greater part of the period under consideration. From the beginning of the Han dynasty till the middle of the Ming, China's population remained more or less constant at the fifty- to sixty-million mark, with the result that for a period of sixteen hundred years there was no serious pressure of population on the land, which in turn meant that the peasantry was able to eke out a tolerable existence.

The amazing constancy of the number of China's population through such a long period of time forms instructive study, especially in view of the change of the ratio of population to land after the Ming dynasty. From the founding of the Han till the beginning of the Sung—that is, roughly from 200 B.C. till A.D. 1000—North China and Central-South China were two separate economic sections. The less fertile north supported its population with its own food supply without drawing upon the potentially rich rice production of the trans-Yangtze region. Inasmuch as Chinese society originated in the north, however, and only very gradually spread southward to the Yangtze and beyond, a preponderant proportion of the Chinese population was to be found in North China from the Han through the T'ang dynasty. (The north-south ratio of the population was 90–10 under the Han; 70–30 under the Tsin; 65–35 under the T'ang.) Only after the wars during the latter part of the T'ang and the disunion following its collapse did the population of North China and Central-South China reach a 50–50 ratio. Because the major concentration of population was in the north up to about A.D. 1000, and because the north suffered from recurrent wars and famine and increasing soil erosion, it was not surprising that the population did not grow to any appreciable extent.

In the Sung dynasty (960–1279), however, the integration of the economy of North and Central China began, as evidenced by the removal of the capital to Kaifeng (in Honan) in order to control the north-south grain transport routes. Moreover, mass migrations of population to the south of the Yangtze took place under the pressure of the Khitan and Juchen invaders in the same period. This great change made it possible for the population of the north to thrive on the food from the south whenever permitted by peace and unification, and at the same time led to the accelerated development of the trans-Yangtze region with the influx of settlers from the north. Central and South

China now witnessed a steady growth of population. North China, on the other hand, suffered greatly from wars and invasions throughout the Sung and Yuan (Mongol) periods. Its population therefore did not register any appreciable growth until peace was restored under the Ming. By the end of the Ming, however, the total population figure reached the hundred-million mark.

Thus, for about sixteen centuries the agrarian population of China, while living under great economic and social injustices, was able to maintain its livelihood without excessive hardship. The pressure of the population on the land had not as yet become critical. With the fall of the Ming, however, the situation changed radically. In 1644 the Manchus conquered China. Known as the Ch'ing dynasty, the Manchus ruled over China for nearly three hundred years, until their regime was overthrown in the Revolution of 1911–12. It was during this period that the crucial change in the Chinese economy took place. The population toward the end of the Ming, as we have seen, stood at approximately 100,000,000. During the first two reigns of the Manchu rule, covering roughly the second half of the seventeenth century, it remained more or less at the same figure. Between 1700 and 1850, however, the population increased by 400 per cent. The country had been enjoying prolonged peace. The national economy was more thoroughly integrated than ever before. The total grain output was further augmented by the planting of new crops introduced from abroad, notably kaoliang and corn, in addition to the staple crops of wheat and rice. Under the combined impact of these factors, the demographic complexion of the country changed from the amazing constancy of the last two millennia to the rapid and sudden bulge of the eighteenth and nineteenth centuries. With this fourfold increase occurring within two centuries (100 million in 1644; 140 million by 1741; and over 400 million by 1850), China became in a very real sense "a country of teeming millions."

The economic and social consequences of such a radical shift in the ratio of population to land cannot be over-emphasized. To begin with, the density of population in cultivated areas suddenly increased. One must remember in this connection that despite such an enormous popula-tion growth, there was little corresponding increase in ag-ricultural acreage and production. For example, in 1701, there were 7½ million ching (a land measurement equiva-lent to about fifteen acres) under cultivation, and in 1793 that number had only increased to 9 million ching. The result was that by the middle of the nineteenth century, eighty per cent of China's population was crowded into less than twenty per cent of her territory. The average per capita landholding was less than four mou, or slightly more than half an acre. One inevitable result was the in-creasing fragmentation of the cultivated areas into tiny farms which reduced the per capita income of the peasants to the bare subsistence, and sometimes starvation, level. Another outcome was a mad scramble for the possession of land. With land increasingly scarce and its value steadily rising, distribution became more and more uneven until a great portion of the productive land was concentrated in the hands of the wealthy landlords, while a large percent-age of the peasant population lost whatever little holdings they had and were reduced to the status of tenants, farm laborers, or paupers. Thus, the chronicles of the reign of Ch'ien Lung, which covered the greater part of the eighteenth century, were replete with these developments: inordinate increase of land values; displacement of large numbers of peasants in crowded areas; a sharp increase in rent demanded by landlords from tenants; scandals in the pre-emption of valuable land by the privileged groups; and further accentuation of agrarian distress as a result of wars against the aborigines in the southwest, which in itself was a movement to open more virgin lands for the expanding population.

Chinese society by the beginning of the nineteenth century, then, was not to be compared with the society of the earlier periods. Although the sociological structure followed a line of remarkable continuity, the spirit of the earlier ages was sedate while that of the nineteenth century was clearly explosive. In earlier times the privileged groups maintained a comfortable margin of advantage over the peasantry, with the result that most peasant revolts were easily suppressed. The striking fact about the social and economic ferment in the nineteenth century was that peasant discontent and rebellions now became increasingly uncontrollable. The privileged groups sought to contain the popular outbreaks, but found their task almost impossible. First came the White Lotus uprising at the end of the eighteenth and the opening of the nineteenth centuries. Then followed the great Taiping and Nien Fei rebellions in the middle of the nineteenth century. In the latter half of the century the country was rudely shocked by a series of Mohammedan revolts in the northwest. The endless chain of popular uprisings showed that the forces of revolution hitherto held in abeyance had now gathered so much momentum that they were irrepressible. The defeat of the Taiping Rebellion by the mobilization of the landlord-scholar class in defense of the old order may be considered as the last victory of the privileged groups against the masses. But in spite of the stubborn gallantry of Tseng Kuo-fan and his associates, the victory solved no problem. Population pressure on the land continued to gain in intensity, and the grievances of the masses against government and privilege continued to mount. The march of the Revolution was only temporarily eclipsed by the failure of the Taipings; it could not be stopped by the reaction.

At this juncture, the impact of foreign imperialism was also felt on a rapidly deteriorating economy. In her encounters with the Western powers from the middle to the end of the nineteenth century, China experienced a round of serious reverses, which reduced her to the status of a semi-colonial country. The extent to which foreign penetration and control through the operation of the unequal treaties and allied instruments contributed to the process of revolution is a matter subject to varying interpretations; but on the whole, the effect of foreign imperialism on the Chinese Revolution appears to have been threefold. First and foremost, the rise of a new class of treaty-port capitalists in the wake of foreign economic influence stimulated the worst kind of landlordism—namely, absentee landlordism. These capitalists, who cornered land and agricultural output with the wealth accumulated under the peculiar trade conditions introduced by the foreign powers were much more exacting than the landlords of the older type. They were the non-tilling landowners or pure rent-collectors, completely ruthless in their exploitation of the peasants. Second, the imperialist powers, prompted by their desire to obtain concessions and motivated by their policy to "divide and rule," indulged in alliances with factional warlords and politicians. Loans were extended to the latter under notorious conditions intended to perpetuate the civil war in China. The dislocations and chaos caused by the unending strife imposed great hardships on the masses and all but ruined the rural economy. Last but not least, the influx of foreign goods, facilitated by the low tariff, virtually destroyed the native village industries. By the first decade of the twentieth century, the various types of foreign economic domination cost China an annual loss of well over a billion dollars. This crushing burden had to be borne by the people, who were already hard-pressed in earning a bare subsistence. No wonder a farsighted thinker warned: "China has reached a state of national bankruptcy, and unless we can save her, economic domination will spell the loss of our country as well as the annihilation of our race."

Only in a negative sense was foreign imperialism a blessing to China: it made the collapse of the *ancien régime* inevitable. Just as the population increase made the suppression of popular revolts a hopeless task, so did the impact of imperialism underscore the absolute need for change. The humiliating defeats that the foreign powers imposed upon China from the Sino-Japanese War in 1894–5 through the Boxer Uprising of 1900–1 exposed the glaring incompetence of the Manchu dynasty. The manner in which the outcome of the Russo-Japanese War (1904–5) violated the territorial integrity of China further emphasized the disintegration of Manchu power. The helplessness of the government in dealing with the foreign powers added cogency to the erupting forces of revolution. Thus during these crucial years when other nations, notably Japan, were modernizing themselves through industrialization, China entered an age of dissolution. The old order broke down at last under the combined weight of great domestic poverty and foreign imperialism. The day of reckoning had arrived, foreshadowing the end of a society and an economy which were over two thousand years old.

It was against this background that the Revolution of 1911 was launched and the Republic brought into being in 1912. The great beacon light during this epoch was Sun Yat-sen. The next twenty years may well be called the Age of Sun. From the historian's standpoint, Sun is the crucial bridge linking the *ancien régime* with the impending onslaught of the Communists. He was prophetic enough to sound the warning and to show the road to constructive action. But as he fathered and revitalized the Kuomintang revolution, he was caught in the vortex of all the retarding influences of dissolution. Following the founding of the Republic, Sun and his colleagues plunged into a veritable "mass of loose sand." The old regime had collapsed, but amidst the debris the conservative forces remained intact. True, both segments of the giant and ancient civilization were moving away from their traditional grooves. True, the Manchu dynasty and all the paraphernalia of absolute monarchy had been done away with. But the challenge of the times was whether the threads of dissolution could be picked up and woven together to create a new base to support a new government. Such a regeneration seemed almost impossible to achieve. Yüan Shih-k'ai and the coterie of Pei-yang generals formed a revival *par excellence* of the rule of the military men. They usurped power to further their personal interests; they employed force to feed their ambition; and they plunged the country into long years of civil war. The landlords and scholars rallied around these

military men just as they had found their way into each
new dynasty in the past. Even the followers of Sun Yat-sen
himself had no true understanding of the revolutionary
faith, much less of democratic government. Their actions
proved that the agelong combination of landlords, scholars, and military men still retained its vigor and sought to
reassert itself in one form or another.

Against this trend of events Sun maintained a vigorous
fight until his death in 1925. The first ten years of the Republic found him nurturing a precarious revolutionary
base in Canton. In point of actual achievement Sun did
very little during this period. His efforts were largely frustrated. But he held fast to his great revolutionary spirit and
vision. In the last five years of his life, he carried out two
major tasks that exerted a continuing influence on the
course of the Chinese Revolution. The first was the sys-
tematization of his revolutionary program in the *San Min
Chu I* (Three People's Principles) ; the second was enlisting the co-operation of the Chinese Communists and the
assistance of Soviet Russia in the reorganization of the
Kuomintang in 1924 in order to put teeth into the Revolution.

The doctrine and program suggested by Sun not only
formed a blueprint for the Kuomintang government in the
next two decades, but contained marked differences from
those subsequently undertaken by the Communists. For
these reasons they are of particular interest. The Revolution as conceived by Sun was to be a multi-pronged movement. First, through the development of Nationalism
(*Min-t'su Chu I*) , the Chinese people were to build a free
and independent nation, which would take its place in the
family of nations on a basis of equality. Then, the political

objective of the Revolution was to attain Democracy (*Min-ch'uan Chu I*) through a gradual process—beginning with the defeat of the warlords, passing through a period of tutelage under the Kuomintang, and culminating in the achievement of constitutional government. The third and perhaps most important aspect of the Revolution—the People's Livelihood (*Min-sheng Chu I*)—was economic and social. Specifically, Sun urged two policies for the *San Min Chu I* state: with respect to agriculture, "land to the cultivator"; and with respect to industrialization, limitation of private capital and development of state capital. In his program of "land to the cultivator," he advocated the adoption of peaceful measures by the government which would enable it to grant or rent land to the landless peasants, to help develop the means of other peasants to purchase land, and to limit the size of holdings of the landlords and compel them to sell surplus land to the small peasants.

In working out this gigantic blueprint for the Chinese Revolution, Sun drew upon the wisdom and experience of both China and the contemporary world. On the one hand, he was anxious to retain traditional Chinese institutions and thinking, while, on the other, he was equally anxious to incorporate the best elements in the experiences of the Western democracies and of Soviet Russia. The concept of "land to the cultivator" had been the one consistent theme in the economic planning of the great statesmen of the past, from Tung Chung-shu onward. Similarly, limitation of private capital had been the main tenet of the progressive school of economic thought, whose protagonists included such men as Sang Hung-yang and Wang An-shih. But admirable as this traditional thinking was, Sun believed that China's political salvation lay in the attainment of democracy, and that her economic revolution should lead to socialism.

Because Sun was aware of the stupendousness of the task, the progress of the Revolution as envisaged by him was intended to be a process of evolution. With the exception of the initial struggle against the warlords, nowhere in Sun's teachings can advocacy of violent means be found. Everywhere the measures he urged look forward to a gradual process of change and progress. Democracy was to be achieved through successive stages. Equalization of land-ownership was to be carried out by legislation for the peaceful transfer of titles rather than by forcible distribution. Sun's entire program thus was characterized by the advocacy of moderate, gradual, and peaceful means. It sought national self-emancipation rather than world revolution; it sought abolition of the unequal treaties rather than anti-imperialism as such; it sought improvement of the people's livelihood through the prevention of the evils of capitalist society rather than through Communism.

Clearly such a program, if and when successfully carried out, would guide China's Revolution along the safest and most useful course. It was in the practical implementation of the program that it left many questions unanswered. In the last analysis, Sun combined in himself the qualities of a great intellectual, a great humanitarian, and a great idealist. Because he was an intellectual, he was able to propound this Magna Charta of the Chinese Revolution. Because he was a humanitarian, he had a deep and sensitive feeling for the welfare of the masses. Because he was an idealist, he maintained a revolutionary vision and zeal which were unfaltering. But Sun was not a practical field worker. He left unanswered the most crucial question: who was going to implement the great doctrine of the People's Livelihood? The privileged groups, firmly entrenched in power, certainly would not initiate this program against their own interests. Neither did he emphasize the precedence of the People's Livelihood over Democracy. To seek political democracy in the absence of the necessary economic conditions is both to waste time and to create chaos. The cynics made a point in ridiculing Sun as *"ch'ih jen shuo meng"* ("madman paraphrasing a dream") .

The argument has sometimes been made that Sun would have done better if he had advanced not all three of his principles, but only the principle of the People's Livelihood; then proper emphasis would have been placed where it belonged. While this view is excessive, it is in accord with the realities of the Chinese Revolution. Sun, in his characteristic utopian fashion, centered his hopes upon progressive social legislation. What he overlooked was the fact that the existing political climate was much too unfavorable for such legislation to become a living force.

In any event, Sun himself soon awakened to the weaknesses of his leadership. The Kuomintang membership was too loose and too heterogeneous. The party organization provided no effective machinery for militant action. Above all, Sun recognized the futility of his struggle without a revolutionary army. As he moved to devise effective methods and weapons to push the Revolution, he embarked on the second of his great tasks: the reorganization of the Kuomintang in 1924 through an entente with Soviet Russia, admission of the Chinese Communists, and an active policy of mass organization. This event was of the greatest importance for future history. As a result of this reorganization, when the Kuomintang underwent an epoch-making revitalization accompanied by the creation of a revolutionary army, the Chinese Revolution entered upon an era of new vigor. The Russian entente and the admission of the Communists contributed to the success of the Northern Expedition of the new revolutionary army. By the spring of 1927, half of the country (south of the Yangtze) had been brought under the control of the revolutionary forces. But at this point there emerged on the Chinese scene a rival formula for the further prosecution of the Revolution. Alongside Sun Yat-sen's *San Min Chu I,* there was now the Communist formula of the Chinese Communist Party. In a sense, the events following the 1924 reorganization of the Kuomintang are a demonstration of the inadequacy of Sun's past strategy and a proof of the great potential strength in Communist revolutionary principles and technique.

China now entered one of the most fateful periods of her history. If Sun had not formed the entente with Soviet Russia or admitted the Communists into the Kuomintang, it is doubtful whether the Northern Expedition would have been successful. Yet the pursuit of these new policies certainly altered the entire outlook of the Chinese Revolution. It is clear that Sun's aim was to enlist the assistance of the Communists in order to hasten the seizure of power, while the direction of the Revolution was to follow the *San Min Chu I* program. As Sun died in 1925, it is futile to conjecture what he would have done had he lived longer. But the assumptions implicit in his stand are significant. For one thing, the Communists were expected to retire or obey the orders of the Kuomintang after the completion of the Northern Expedition. Furthermore, it was taken for granted that the Kuomintang members would be unfailing supporters of his *San Min Chu I* program. It soon became evident that both were too much to expect.

As events unfolded, first with the Communist ascendancy in Wuhan in 1926–7, and later with the new government in Nanking and the launching of the anti-Communist drive led by General Chiang Kai-shek, neither of the two assumptions materialized. The Communists would not meekly submit to the authority of the Kuomintang. The *quid pro quo* for their contribution to the Revolution was no less than the overthrow of the Kuomintang itself. *"Hsing hsing chih huo, k'o yi liao yuan"* ("A flickering spark can engulf the entire plain") —this was the threat to the Chinese Revolution following the admission of the Communists. The Kuomintang, on its part, soon proved itself to be neither willing nor able to carry out the *San Min Chu I* program in accordance with the spirit of Sun. Out of the tangled developments of 1927–8 it became evident that the Chinese Revolution, just brought to new life, was hopelessly split between two extremes: the Communists heading toward the extreme Left, and the Kuomintang toward the extreme Right. The net result was two decades of bitter fighting between the two irreconcilable camps. As far as Sun's *San Min Chu I* was concerned, it fell into a complete vacuum.

The period immediately following the Nanking-Wuhan split of 1927 witnessed the growth of the power of the Nanking government and the temporary eclipse of the Communists. From Wuhan the Communists had made their program known to the public. Unlike the *San Min Chu I* program, it called for class struggle, for the use of violent means, for the practice of Communism, and for an all-out crusade against imperialism as a step toward world revolution. When they were driven underground by the Nanking government, there to re-think their stratagem and to recoup their fortunes, great capital was made of the Communist program to justify Nanking's own turn to the extreme Right.

It is in this violent change of policy that Sun Yat-sen's program was robbed of whatever vitality it possessed at the time of the establishment of the Nanking government. Irreparable harm was done in this way to the *San Min Chu I* principles, and thus to General Chiang's own leadership of the Revolution. Chiang was to head the new Kuomintang government for the next two decades, but, swept by the passion for crushing Communism, the Nanking government went farther than was necessary to cement alliances with the forces of the old society. Up to the split with Wuhan, the grip of the landlords, financiers, and scholar-politicians on the Kuomintang was just beginning to take hold. From 1928 onward, the entry of these elements into influential positions in government assumed alarming proportions. What began as a holy crusade against Communist heresy was conveniently transformed into a full-fledged reaction. Rallied to the support of General Chiang was a splendid galaxy of groups of privilege—landlords and old-time politicians; party bosses, elders, and the ultra-conservative Western Hills group; bankers, financiers, and businessmen; and reformed warlords as well as revolutionary veterans. Against this formidable combination, the opposition of Wang Ching-wei and his followers, who tried to defend Sun's principles, proved to be of no avail. Before long it became evident that this was a re-enactment of the familiar pattern observed during the change of regimes in China's past history.

In theory, *San Min Chu I* remained the exalted program of the Kuomintang government. But what China needed besides a new program was a new birth. Without a new birth, a new program would have no life. The new birth, however, was not forthcoming. The militarist-landlord-scholar combination might employ slogans of the ultramodern type, but their inner spirit was the spirit of their forebears in the days of the absolute monarchy. As in all previous decades of instability, the military men took law and government into their own hands and sacrificed principles to serve their private interests. Semi-independent regimes again appeared in different provinces. Around these military men—"men of real strength," as they were called—the landlords and scholar-officials created alliances and counter-alliances. What need was there of so many cliques if each of them was composed of loyal supporters of *San Min Chu I,* as they professed themselves to be? The central government endeavored to unify the country, but the more it tried, the harder the task became. The blame could hardly be placed on any one particular person, but must be shared by all. The truth of the matter was that the old groups were still trying to rule as they always had in the past; and there was no broad base of popular support on which the *San Min Chu I* state could thrive and grow.

The two decades of General Chiang's ascendancy were marked by a great concentration of the nation's energies and resources in maintaining the Kuomintang position by means of military and political power, to the neglect of the economic and social program, which, in fact, was the only program that could give it real strength. A great hue and cry was raised about Kuomintang tutelage, which was to introduce preparatory steps for democracy. The campaign for the abolition of the unequal treaties was pushed with great publicity. But neither drive had any substantial success, because the basic needs of the people were not met, and the government consequently could not achieve that real strength which could come only from nationwide support. What the nation really witnessed was the use of great military power by General Chiang to enforce the authority of Nanking, and the struggle of the politicians and the privileged groups to gain power and to promote their respective interests. Thus unification was only nominal. Regional warlords openly challenged the central government. The party was torn by factional strife, as secession movements appeared time and again in the southern capital of Canton.

The degree to which the government remained fixed in its indifference to the needs of the masses was indeed astonishing. It showed a strong desire for reconstruction and modernization, but whatever progress was made in this direction was intended primarily to strengthen the power of the ruling circles. As far as the fundamental problem of the well-being of the masses was concerned, it had neither the resolve nor the drive to tackle it. The cause of this withering of the revolutionary spirit was the inability of the government to bridge the gap between itself and the bulk of the population in the countryside. As in earlier ages, the Kuomintang ruled the countryside through an alliance with the landlord class. At this telling level of government—from the hsien (county) downward into the villages—all power, political, economic, judicial, and police, was in the hands of the landlord class. The Kuomintang depended on their co-operation to collect taxes, to maintain order, and to direct the village government. On the two counts that vitally affected the masses—taxation and local village government—there was neither justice nor popular representation. But most serious of all was the failure of the Kuomintang to carry out an effective program for land reform. From all available evidences, the Kuomintang had a great opportunity to put land reform into effect. Had it done this, it would have won the support of the masses, and true unification and peace would have followed. But the groups in control were opposed to social change. Without social change there could be no improvement in the standard of living of the people. This was the fatal weakness of the Kuomintang government.

In our discussion of Sun Yat-sen's teachings I have mentioned that unless there is adequate safeguard for implementation, well-conceived principles usually end in failure. Land reform did indeed receive the attention of the legislators. The law passed by Nanking provided for the lowering of farm rents to 37½ per cent of the crop yield, the abolition of subtenancy, and the right of perpetual lease. But it remained on the books without being enforced. The landlords continued to collect rents which ranged as high as 50 to 70 per cent, exacting as much as they could get. The impact of this state of affairs on the peasant population was far-reaching. For the government to pass a progressive measure and then fail to keep its pledge to the people by enforcing it appeared to be adding insult to injury in the eyes of the masses.

Months and years went by with the Nanking government held captive by the old groups that strove to retain power and to obstruct measures for economic and social change. The Kuomintang's historic mission was to exercise tutelage and to introduce constitutional government. But without a social transformation, there was no new class to set democracy going. To give life to tutelage (which meant preparation for democracy) and constitutional government (which meant the maturing of democracy) required the stimulus born of a responsive political consciousness among the masses plus able leadership from those who were loyal to *San Min Chu I* in word and in deed. That neither existed was the basic reason why the Kuomintang government could not hold its own. The Kuomintang was created and nurtured by Sun Yat-sen with the express hope that it would carry out *San Min Chu I* in accordance with the true spirit of his teachings, thereby leading the Chinese Revolution to its triumph. But it dissipated valuable time during its tenure of office without accomplishing anything toward the realization of Sun's program.

It was during these crucial years that the Communists took upon themselves the role of championing the much needed economic and social revolution. After their rout in 1927, the evolution of the Communist movement came about in a quiet, unheralded, but most forceful fashion. Its rise almost precisely paralleled the weakening of the Kuomintang. While the Kuomintang lost its opportunity to lead the *San Min Chu I* revolution, the Communists made ready to carry out their own program.

It must be said that within the Communist leadership at this time there was by no means unanimity of view. A process of selection and elimination intervened. But before long the older schools, which believed either in meek co-operation with the Kuomintang or in uprisings by urban workers, gave way to the new leadership, which, under the guidance of Mao Tse-tung, shifted emphasis to the organization of the peasantry as the revolutionary base. Thus, at last, China's economic and social revolution found its sponsor, and could burst forth with explosive power.

In a very real sense, the failure of the Kuomintang was responsible for the success of this new group of Communist leaders. The secret of the Kuomintang's weakness was understood better and sooner by the latter than by the Kuomintang members themselves. The Communists, by watching the Kuomintang performance, found that to grope within the limitations set by Kuomintang methods would not meet the needs of the people. In an underdeveloped country like China, the quest for democracy of the Western type provided no safeguards against abuse by the leaders in power and could only result in continuing the empty forms of the preceding years. They further believed that the power structure in Nanking, a repetition of the evils of past dynasties, would only worsen with time, as the clash of the Kuomintang dictatorship and the interests of the masses came into sharp focus. The basic trouble with the Kuomintang, in their opinion, was that all its efforts were directed toward a struggle for power within the privileged groups, while the land and peasant problem, the most urgent of all revolutionary tasks, was left untouched. Such insight into the logic of the times molded a new body of revolutionary ideas and tactics in the minds of Mao and his associates. Within a surprisingly short period of time, these crystallized into a program of action whose central thesis—directly opposed to that of the Kuomintang—was that the only potential base for an effective revolutionary government was in the vast agricultural population. Accordingly, without losing time, the Communists set out to put their program to a practical test in the agricultural heartland of central China.

The result was immediate and startling. The latent power in this great human reservoir responded almost instantly to the tapping by the Communist leaders. They quickly discovered that not only could they regain the ground lost in 1927 but they could expand their strength on a vast and lasting basis by focusing all strategy to accord with their new insight into the almost limitless explosive force in the economic and social revolution. In the agrarian revolution they launched in the rural border areas of Kiangsi and Hunan, the peasants were given a leadership and an organization that were without precedent in history. Grievances were actively built up against the village bosses as well as against the rule of the gentry in combination with the *tangpu* (local Kuomintang party headquarters), the telling level at which the Kuomintang failed to offer a satisfactory program to the masses in the countryside. After the existing power structure was broken, the Communists organized local government by soviets, wherein the poor and landless peasants were given the major voice; they distributed land taken from the landlords to this rural proletariat. Most important of all, along with these radical reforms, the peasants were organized into a Red Army. This welded together the Communists' political and military power and created an integrated weapon of assault for the emancipated peasants as a class against all the privileged groups of the country.

This tremendous social transformation marked the beginning of what is now known as the Mao Tse-tung line. The policy basis of this line is best stated in Mao's own words: "The principle of the land policy of the Soviet is to wipe out completely feudalistic and semi-feudalistic oppression and exploitation. . . . Our class line in the agrarian revolution is to depend upon the hired farm hands and poor peasants, to ally with the middle peasants, to check the rich peasants, and to annihilate the landlords. The correct practice of this line is the key to the success of the agrarian revolution and the foundation for all other policies of the Soviet government in the villages." From the standpoint of strategy, the Mao line is composed of these ingredients: land reform, a strong political party, a Red Army, and a self-supporting territorial base, usually located in "border areas" astride interprovincial boundaries.

In subsequent years there has been a tendency in Chinese Communist Party circles to exalt the wisdom of Mao Tse-tung. In other quarters, there has been criticism of Mao as a deviationist from Marxism-Leninism. As a matter of fact, to view Mao either as infallible or as a heretic misses the main point of his importance as a revolutionary leader. Mao's chief claim to greatness does not lie in his originality or in his capacity for minute analysis. It lies rather in the directness of his observation and thinking, and the pertinence of his conclusions to the realities confronting him.

The idea of a peasant proletariat which underlies the entire body of Mao's revolutionary ideas and tactics, is a strictly hybrid product. A great part of Mao's thinking as well as his methods of organization are no doubt inspired by Marxist and Leninist teachings. But equally important as sources of Mao's inspiration has been the stream of proletarian literature handed down through the ages in

China and the doctrine of the People's Livelihood of Sun Yat-sen himself. Mao's thorough and shrewd understanding of the temperament and needs of the Chinese masses and his downright ruggedness in championing the cause of the underdog or the social outcast are traceable to such popular novels as the *Shui Hu Chuan* (*All Men Are Brothers*). It is this stream of popular literature that helped to develop in Mao's thinking a particular pertinence to the realities of Chinese society. On the other hand, if Sun Yat-sen's doctrine of the People's Livelihood ever had a thorough convert, that convert was Mao Tsetung himself. More than anybody else, Mao took Sun's exhortations to heart. It is interesting to recall in this connection that it was Sun Yat-sen who declared that the economic and social objectives of the Chinese Revolution were not unlike the objectives of Communism, but, given the unique conditions of China, the Chinese revolutionaries "should follow Marx in general principle but must not slavishly copy his methods." If Mao is the inventor of a new Asian version of Communism, as is often maintained nowadays, Sun Yat-sen certainly was the harbinger who blazed the trail for him. Mao is thus the greatest eclectic among the world's revolutionary leaders. What makes him stand above other eclectics is his ability to digest the thinking of great men of different lands and ages, weave them into an integral but workable whole, and shape the resultant strategy into a militant weapon for spearheading the Chinese Revolution.

In any event, within the short span of a few years, the strength of the Chinese Soviet Republic in Central China spoke for itself. General Chiang Kai-shek, mobilizing the major resources of the Nanking government, launched six great campaigns to "suppress the Communist bandits." Yet the peasant revolution had already struck such deep root among the masses that in spite of the superior manpower and arms of Nanking, the Communist regime could not be wiped out. For the first time, a Chinese military leader found not only that he was leading his army to join battle with another army but that he was confronting an army plus the hostile population of the entire countryside. Each victory scored by the Kuomintang forces was followed by the resurgence of fresh sectors of enemy strength. Juichin, the capital of the Soviet state, looked so near, and yet it was so far to reach. When at last the Red government and the Red Army were dislodged from Central China, there still was no real extermination of the Communists. The widespread revolutionary forces engendered by the Mao Tse-tung line enabled the Communists to undertake the historic Long March to northern Shensi and to resume their operations in that northwestern "border area." There, with Yenan as their capital, the Communists pursued on a more extended scale and with renewed vigor their unfinished tasks begun in Central China.

The events that took place in the 1930's may be said to be the first round in the Communist challenge to the Kuomintang. Following the dislodgment of the Communists from Kiangsi, the question arose as to what the Nanking government was going to do with the land redistribution and other revolutionary measures carried out by the Reds. It could either recognize them or repudiate them. Nanking chose the latter. The drastic restoration of landlords and other ante-bellum conditions in the areas retaken from the Communists proved how shortsighted the Kuomingtang policy was. It alienated the masses completely. It strengthened the Communist case. It induced the peasants, including even those who were opposed to the methods of the Kiangsi soviets, to become Red converts. While this policy of the Kuomintang played directly into the hands of the Communists, Nanking held on to a false sense of security by speaking in terms of the complete eradication of the Red menace in two or three years. Nothing could have been further from the truth. The Reds, far from being defeated, were opening a new page in the expansion of their influence. Hitherto, their influence was concentrated in Central China, the heartland of Chinese agriculture. Now they were compelled to carry their revolutionary program into North China and Manchuria, where the social upheaval had scarcely begun. Thus the removal to Yenan, while outwardly a setback in Communist strength, in reality helped to broaden Communist influence on a scale much greater than that of the Kiangsi days.

With Yenan, accordingly, began a new phase in the Communist challenge to the Kuomintang. It seemed that the initiative forfeited by the Kuomintang had passed directly into the hands of the Communists. The formula was almost incredibly simple. The Kuomintang neglected the People's Livelihood; the Communists blessed it with ever-increasing attention. One was solidly aligned with the privileged groups; the other was entirely free from them. By doing everything that the Kuomintang failed or refused to do, the Communists identified themselves with the needs of the masses with unprecedented ease and success. In these years, then, the forces of China's economic and social revolution turned away from the Kuomintang and bowed to the leadership of the Communists.

The completion of the Long March, despite the most

adverse circumstances, demonstrated that the Red Star was far from waning. One advantage afforded by Yenan was that the widely scattered pockets of Communist strength now converged there, to make it the Mecca of the next phase of the struggle. Another advantage was its relative remoteness from the center of Kuomintang military power, for in the northwest the strength of Nanking's unification was thinnest and the Communists could enjoy a breathing spell to regroup themselves. Still another outcome was that in an intangible way Yenan attracted to its support more non-Communist sympathizers than did Juichin.

None the less, the hardships faced by Yenan were tremendous. The remaining units of the Red Army were all but shattered. The moral support of the politically articulate sections of the country did not bring the much needed money or food or arms to this bleak northwestern retreat to help rebuild the Communist forces. Nanking, while farther away than before, mobilized the Northeastern troops to attempt a death blow to the precarious new base. Worst of all, the Shensi-Kansu border area, celebrated for its herbs but of little importance for staple agricultural production, was ill suited for carrying out the same agrarian revolution as had been practiced in Central China. In Central China, tenant farmers with no land at all formed over 50 per cent of the rural population, while in North China they represented only about 25 per cent. The evils of landlordism were not so grievous as those in the crowded belts of Central China, and consequently the masses were much less responsive to calls for armed rebellion. In view of these limitations, it was evident that the Kiangsi formula would not produce the same effectiveness in this region. The Communists saw a way out in the broad plains

of North China, but the area could hardly be brought under control unless the Kuomintang military threat could
be stayed first.

Under these circumstances, the adoption of a new strategy became a compelling necessity. This was the period, it
may be recalled, when the threat of large-scale Japanese
invasion was approaching the zero hour. The Kuomintang
was caught between the Communists in its rear and the
Japanese on its front doorstep. Had it followed a program
of vigorous economic and social reform, it could have resisted both menaces. But since no reforms were forthcoming, not only was the success in Kiangsi a Pyrrhic victory,
but large sections of public opinion were rising in condemnation of the government's appeasement policy toward
Japan. As a result, Nanking could not resist Japan for fear
of the Communist menace in the rear; neither could it concentrate on the extinction of the Communist influence for
fear of completely losing popular support. This was the
situation when the Communist leaders sought a new strategy to cope with Nanking.

Whatever their merits or demerits may be, the historian
must give due credit to the Communist leaders for their
resourcefulness of mind and boldness of policy-concep-
tion. The Communists temporarily relegated their agrarian revolution to a secondary place and pursued a new
plan in an effort to avert the new series of anti-Communist campaigns initiated by General Chiang Kai-shek.
Accordingly, they greatly exploited the issue of resistance to Japan and the need for a united front against
foreign aggression. Prior to this the Communists had gone
on record with a token declaration of war against Japan
(1932); a manifesto on an anti-Japanese united front

(1933); and a call for an all-class stand against Japan (1934). But now from Yenan, a new drive was launched to magnify the issue of a united front. In August 1935 a declaration was issued calling for the establishment of an Anti-Japanese National United Front. The slogan: "Chinese do not fight Chinese," sent its echoes throughout the four corners of the country. Such a move, in the opinion of the Red leaders, would produce certain major consequences. First, it would seize the initiative momentarily from the hands of the Kuomintang. Second, it would make Nanking's anti-Communist campaign so unpopular that it might backfire. Third, by appealing to the patriotism of all segments of Chinese society instead of repeating the "class line" of the Kiangsi days, it would win tremendous support in North China and Manchuria as well as throughout the rest of China. If war with Japan failed to materialize, Nanking would be more and more discredited. If it did break out, then the Communists would have a grand opportunity once again to carry out their agrarian revolution. Such was the true background of the campaign for the united front. As it turned out, the movement looked like part of a world-wide popular-front line. But the changed environment of the Communists in the northwest and the need to stay Nanking's impending campaigns were the chief motivating factors.

The united-front drive, however, did not immediately bear fruit. While the country was bombarded with all manner of propaganda by the National Salvationists and the Democratic League as well as the Communists, General Chiang ordered the Northeastern Army to prepare for renewed drives against northern Shensi. "Unification before resistance" was the policy of Nanking. Faced with such a situation, the Communists realized that the campaign for a united front had to be reinforced by bold and swift action. The new plan as finally worked out embraced two steps: first, to infiltrate the Northeastern Army mobilized by General Chiang to fight the Communists and to fraternize with the troops; then to resort to a desperate plot to force Chiang to accept the Communist terms under the threat of death. The kidnapping of the Generalissimo at Sian by mutinous troops in December 1936 must be considered as one of the most sensational extortion cases in history. Whatever technicalities may absolve the Communists from duplicity in the plot, the incontrovertible fact is that the *coup de théâtre* followed in direct line the truce they had established with the rebel troops. It is true that the Communists played a decisive role in the ultimate safe release of General Chiang. But *"chieh ling huan shih chi ling jen"* ("the one who loosened the bell was the one who originally tied it!") . The life of the captive was spared with a major political objective: only Chiang's prestige could make possible the momentous decision to throw the Kuomintang forces into an all-out war with Japan, which the Communists desperately wished to happen. It was by these tactics, strongly reminiscent of Chinese Robin Hoods of bygone ages but carried out with the masterly perfection of a twentieth-century coup, that the Communists once again stabilized their power and opened the way to carry out the Revolution in North China.

From the dramatic Sian incident onward, one event after another widened the advantage of the Communists over the Kuomintang. The Sian incident was in reality a turning-point in China's destiny. When General Chiang yielded to the terms of the rebels (as in fact he did), the seed was sown for the doom of the Kuomintang in 1949. The armistice with the Reds meant a new lease of life and a new period for their expansion in North China. More significant still, it committed Chiang to turn his forces against the Japanese. This meant the certain decimation of the Kuomintang army. The war with Japan broke out seven months after the Sian incident. Within one year the cream of the Kuomintang forces was destroyed in engagements with the Japanese army. From this point on, the mortal threat to the Communists ceased to exist.

The agreement between the Communists and the Kuomintang for the cessation of the civil war and for a joint war effort against the Japanese was at best a nominal accord. Neither side trusted the other; both made use of the next eight years to build bases for postwar power. In this race for future supremacy, the Kuomintang lost out entirely to the Communists. From the time Chu Teh and P'eng Teh-huai led the Eighth Route Army into northern Hopei and Shansi, and Lin Piao scored the victory at Ping-hsing-kuan (September 1937) until Japan's surrender (August 1945), the Communist power spread from the Shensi-Kansu-Ninghsia Border Region into Hopei, Shansi, Honan, Shantung, Hupeh, Manchuria, Suiyuan, Chahar, Jehol, and the lower Yangtze region. The Kuomintang forces, on the other hand, after suffering heavy casualties in the Shanghai battles, lost Nanking, Hsuchow, Hankow, and Canton in rapid succession and were forced to retreat westward into the southwestern provinces, with Chungking (in Szechuan) as the new capital. From the standpoint of the struggle for power, the years of the war were certainly put to excellent use by the Communists, while the Kuomintang suffered greatly on account of its inability to revitalize itself in the western hinterland.

The decade of the extension of Communist power in the midst of war forms interesting study. A basis for free expansion was provided by the removal of the military power of Nanking, for which the Communists had worked indefatigably ever since their march to Yenan. Now that this objective had been achieved, they turned their efforts to the problem of contending with the Japanese invaders. For this they quickly evolved effective methods. The approach to the new problem was not unlike the approach used in the Kiangsi days—that is, a reliance upon the organization of the masses. But the details of the strategy were different. Instead of confiscating the land of all landlords, they only stripped financial power from the absentee or non-tilling landlords. In the case of the operating or resident landlords, they merely reduced the proportion of the crop exacted from the tenants as rent. Similarly, interest rates in the villages were decreased. Then a mild form of village self-government was carried out. Instead of using the poor and landless peasants to form soviets, all classes, excepting of course the disowned landlords, were included in village elections for the local councils. The overriding Communist policy was to be content with a moderate version of agrarian revolution, but to keep it sufficiently effective so that the large sectors of rural population benefiting from the reforms would be eager to accept Communist leadership. Such prudence was immediately rewarded. The masses behind the enemy lines responded to Communist direction just as they did in the Kiangsi days.

In time this gave the Communists control of extensive

areas. The cities and rail lines held by the Japanese invaders were constantly exposed to attack by guerrilla bands led by the Communists. The successful utilization of guerrilla warfare was much more than a matter of military strategy. Reference has been made to this type of fighting in Kiangsi. Now, on a much larger scale, it was applied to the Japanese. The vitality of the guerrillas lay in the social upheaval which mobilized the countryside to work together with the fighting men. It was the crystallization of a dynamic social transformation that enabled the Communists to extend their power as they did. Historically, when China was confronted by invaders, the response of the Chinese government was either resistance with regular armies, appeasement, or surrender. For the first time, the Communists developed the new formula of using guerrilla warfare to strike behind the enemy lines. Such a unique strategy was certainly no accident. The Communists could carry it out because they had mastered the key for winning the cooperation of the countryside.

Meantime, the spectacle presented in the Kuomintang areas of the southwest formed a direct contrast. The government in Chungking found itself detached from the original base of its resources in the seaboard provinces. If it had chosen to correct its past error of neglecting the masses, a new role of leadership would have been developed, as the nationwide mobilization enlarged the revolutionary mission of the war and gave General Chiang broad wartime powers for mass organization. The task of organizing a new and vigorous base in the southwestern hinterland, however, was beset with difficulties. The domination of the privileged groups in the province of Szechuan, for instance, was even more tenacious than that in the lower

Yangtze provinces. On the other hand, the war imposed its inevitable demands for sacrifice upon the people. The government needed more revenue; the army needed more men and more food. A shortage of production and a rise in prices were almost unavoidable. Without radical changes in the social structure, such demands could not be satisfied, and trouble continued to mount. Unable to alter the existing situation, the Kuomintang once again aligned itself with the privileged groups and pursued a rickety course of continuing the resistance under the many trying circumstances created by the war.

In a sense, the Chungking government in these years suggests the refugee regimes under the Eastern Tsin (A.D. 317–420) and the Southern Sung (1127–1279) dynasties. Having lost its old base of operation, the refugee regime in Chungking, like those of earlier periods, found revival extremely difficult. Corruption overtook the rank and file of the government. Persons of influence turned to graft, profiteering, and the pursuit of political power. Runaway inflation and soaring prices became the order of the day, while wartime profits were concentrated in the hands of a few at the top. The masses bore with the government as long as both shared the misfortunes of the war. But the fabulous wealth of certain leaders set against the abject poverty of the people formed a shocking commentary on a government whose object was to lead the nation to victory against the Japanese. Just as under the Eastern Tsin and the Southern Sung, there was a loud outcry of irredentism, but the strength was lacking to implement so high-spirited an emotion. The outcome was that while Communist power steadily grew, the Kuomintang war effort developed an increasing reliance not upon itself but upon

Allied help. The Kuomintang now found itself in a greater predicament than ever before. Because it had failed all along to organize for mass support, the extension of Communist strength aroused in it an increasing fear. The race for postwar supremacy was going more and more in favor of the Communists.

About midway in the war with Japan, Chungking became so alarmed over Communist expansion into enemy-occupied areas that reports of renewed civil war spread. In Shensi, too, the Kuomintang instituted a blockade attempting to throttle the source of Communist power. This, however, was a futile measure, for it did not stem the tide of Communist expansion. At the same time the Kuomintang itself never succeeded in erecting its own cells of strength behind the enemy lines. It is often said that the reason for this failure was the lack of interest among the Kuomintang generals in the development of large guerrilla units for fear that these units might eventually threaten their vested interests. But this was not the entire truth. The Kuomintang armies did not win over the population of the countryside; and without the dynamic forces of social transformation, guerrillas could not be created.

In January 1940 Mao Tse-tung came forth with his ringing document *On New Democracy*. This was, in effect, the declaration of a new stage in the Communist challenge to the Kuomintang. No longer stressing the united front with the Kuomintang, the Communists were now strong enough to put forth their bid for power. Mao's central theme was that the current stage of the Chinese Revolution should no longer be bourgeois-led or bourgeois-controlled, but should rather be led by the "joint dictatorship of several revolutionary classes." This was the new form of revolutionary dictatorship which Mao claimed he had discovered as particularly suited to a semi-colonial country like China, which had to go through a transitional stage in the absence of a "proletarian dictatorship." In practical application, *On New Democracy* was a grand rationalization meant to justify the Communists' determination to overthrow the Kuomintang and to seize total power.

The last four years of the war witnessed a rapid increase in Communist strength. By 1944, some nineteen "Liberated Areas" (Communist-controlled areas), with a total population of one hundred million, stretched from Inner Mongolia in the north to Hainan Island in the south. The regular Red armed forces were about one million strong, while the People's Militia numbered about two million. Toward the close of 1944, Communist political demands became more extensive and uncompromising. At the third session of the People's Political Council in Chungking, they pressed for the end of the Kuomintang dictatorship and the creation of a coalition government. What the Communists were asking was no less than the voluntary abdication of the Kuomintang government and the creation of a "joint dictatorship of several revolutionary classes," with the Communists at the top. When this was rejected by the Kuomintang and negotiations became deadlocked, Mao Tse-tung went one step farther to reaffirm his demand by issuing another important document, *On Coalition Government* (April 1945). The demands made on the Kuomintang were three pages long. The list reminded one strikingly of the "Seven Hates," a proclamation of deep-seated grievances set forth by Nurhachi, the Manchu conqueror of China, in the early seventeenth century. The two documents—*On New Democracy* and *On Coalition Government*—form a complete sequence: the broad principles advanced in the first were spelled out in concrete demands in the second.

When the war with Japan ended in August 1945, the final act in the contest for power between the Communists and the Kuomintang was immediately joined. In this gigantic struggle the Kuomintang was clearly no match for the Communists. It was not that the Communists were superior to the Kuomintang in military strength. In fact, the regular Communist army was inferior in numbers, and certainly the Kuomintang had a decisive advantage in the great quantities of military equipment which it received from the United States. But what made the Communists invincible was the fact that they had gained control of a large portion of China's vast countryside and had successfully aroused the peasants and organized them for action, while the groups in control of the Kuomintang had lost their old bases and were unable to create new strength. This situation was thoroughly appreciated by the Communists when in 1946 they were asked to enter into peace talks and accept the mediation of the special American envoy, General George Marshall. Throughout these conferences the Communists had no real desire to come to any settlement with the Kuomintang short of a complete acceptance of their own terms. They were confident of their ultimate victory. The fact that the talks were drawn out for over a year meant only that the Communists needed time to prepare for the final showdown. It was no wonder, then, when the great civil war came in 1947–9, that the Kuomintang found itself with an opponent whose sharp cutting edge it could not match. When the debacle finally came, the dissolution of the Kuomintang regime on the mainland of China was as speedy as it was irrevocable.

From the standpoint of the historian, the Communist victory represents a great landmark in the destiny of the Chinese people. The point of departure was the crystallization and application of the Mao Tse-tung line. It was Mao's particular theories and stratagem that wrote finis to the structure of China's traditional society. The old society had been tottering long before the advent of Mao, but its component parts sought to function in their habitual grooves. After Mao launched the agrarian revolution and built up the Red Army, the break with the *ancien régime* was complete. In this dramatic rendezvous with destiny, the dormant forces of a great economic and social revolution and the Communist leadership converged to introduce a new age in Chinese history.

II

THE FOUNDATIONS OF COMMUNIST
STRENGTH AND SUCCESS

❁

IF the irrepressible Revolution described above provided the basis for the upheaval in China, certainly the role played by the Communists has led that Revolution to its climax. It is, of course, too early to see what lasting effect the regime in Peking will have on the happiness and welfare of the Chinese people. The success of the Communists in establishing themselves as the leaders of the Revolution, however, is an indisputable fact. They have constituted the largest single force in mobilizing, developing, and directing the nascent energies of the new age. It is therefore important to examine the fundamental reasons for the strength and success of the Communist movement.

The Chinese Communists began their career in the 1920's under the powerful influence of Borodin, Blücher, and others. The impact of these veteran revolutionary workers, fresh from the new Russia of the Bolshevik Revolution, upon the young Chinese Communist Party was tremendous. These men brought to Canton the entire apparatus of Russian revolutionary doctrine and technique and demonstrated its operation to the Chinese Communists. The impression of this know-how on the minds of these young zealots was as profound as it was dramatic.

It was Borodin and his colleagues who insisted upon the importance of mass organization as a revolutionary weapon. The peasant and labor departments in the government in Canton were then headed by members of the Communist Party. Through these persons Borodin left a legacy that greatly influenced the trend of future events. At the plenary sessions of the Kuomintang in 1926–7, Borodin repeatedly urged the policy of land confiscation. While the plan was defeated upon the strenuous objection of Wang-Ching-wei, it left an indelible impression on the Communist members. Borodin was also behind the Hongkong-Shameen strike of 1925–6 (directed against the British) and the organization of the Union of Military Youth (a clique of Communist "activists" in the revolutionary army). These incidents served to demonstrate the technique of an anti-imperialist crusade as well as the "planting of illegal fighting apparatus within the Kuomintang." In all spheres of activity the guiding hand of Borodin pointed the way.

It was in the summer of 1927 that Borodin and the Communists were expelled from the Kuomintang in Wuhan. But the three and a half years of intensive training received by the Chinese Communists left a lasting imprint on their thinking. It is important to remember that the Communists exposed to Borodin's influence at that time were in the most formative years of their lives. Nothing, not even the writings of Marx, Lenin, and Stalin, could have impressed them more deeply than the visible doings of these professional revolutionaries working in their midst. Among the fundamental concepts advanced by Borodin during these years were those advocating a radical government based upon peasant and labor unions, the maintenance of close relations with Moscow, non-with-drawal from the Kuomintang but subversion from within, and the ultimate seizure of power. Mere agrarian reform without the seizure of power was never intended to be the goal. One cannot but be struck by the persistence of this line of thinking in the program of Mao Tse-tung in later years. To be sure, the crowded events of the intervening years required many revisions in Borodin's instructions, but it is an indisputable fact that the first driving force in the Chinese Communist movement was sparked by the teachings and concrete field operations of these Russian advisers.

While the young comrades of China became the willing converts of their Russian mentors, they were in another sense highly iconoclastic. Being for the most part intellectuals and students, the Chinese Communist leaders in those early years went through a continuous process of dissent and counter-dissent. The result was the evolution and establishment of an effective line of action, or of the "correct line" as it is now called, which guided them to the portals of success. The earliest leader of the Chinese Communist movement was Ch'en Tu-hsiu, a man who believed that the Chinese Revolution should be led by the bourgeoisie and that the proletariat should content itself with the preservation of its rights. Later, their leader was Ch'ü Ch'iü-pai, who advocated revolutionary uprisings at all costs, deprecated any kind of retreat, and as a result led the party to perilous sacrifices. Following Ch'ü were Li Li-san who overestimated the power of the uprisings by urban workers, and Chang Kuo-t'ao, who, "never seeing the peasants but only seeing the laborers," believed that the Revolution should not be based on agrarian support.

These schools of thought were overcome one after another by the thinking of Mao Tse-tung. As early as February 1927, in his report on the peasant movement in
Hunan, Mao brought forth his program for agrarian revolution. This program he continued to elaborate during the
next decade, urging its adoption as the guiding strategy of
the Communist Party. Mao refused to submit to the leadership of the Kuomintang as Ch'en urged, nor did he wish
to close the door to co-operation with the Kuomintang
as Chang advised. Most emphatically, he deplored the
"putschism" of Ch'ü and the suicidal policy of fomenting
urban uprisings pursued by Li. This series of battles in
revolutionary doctrine waged by Mao against his co-
workers was perhaps what saved the Chinese Communist
movement. It is to be recalled that the disconnected
threads of Borodin's influence had been confusing, and
that the clash of different factions, each claiming some
authority but none meeting the needs of the time, simply
sapped the strength of the party. Mao's thesis cleared the
air and coalesced the scattered brands of thinking into a
consistent body of revolutionary doctrine. He urged that
emphasis be placed on the organization of the peasant
masses as the only effective revolutionary base. He drew
attention to the importance of the poor and landless peasants in particular as a reservoir of revolutionary strength.
He stressed the necessity of establishing rural self-government and arming the emancipated peasants. The far-reaching consequences of the Mao Tse-tung line have already
been dealt with in the preceding chapter. What should be
stressed here is that it was developed after a period of failure and dissent, and for that reason became the rallying-
point of all subsequent revolutionary effort. This goes a

long way to explain why the leadership wielded by Mao was remarkably free from disintegrating forces.

Mao propounded his thesis in 1927, but it was not until 1935 that he became the formally recognized leader of the Chinese Communist Party. At the halfway point, late in 1931, he was made chairman of the government of the Chinese Soviet Republic, which had just been formed by the First All-China Congress of the Soviets. What happened in the interval between 1927 and 1935 was illustrative of another important aspect of the evolution of personalities and policies inside the Communist Party. During these years Mao was admittedly a junior member among the Communist leaders. His recommendations for concentrating the party's efforts on peasant organization received only scant attention. But two factors militated in his favor. The pertinence of his views on the necessity of a peasant revolutionary base soon became indisputable. Added to this, he and his close associates went directly into the field to put the idea of peasant revolution into actual operation. Although the Nanchang uprising of August 1, 1927, led by Chu Teh, Chou En-lai, Yeh T'ing, and Ho Lung, and the Autumn Harvest insurrection in Hunan in September 1927, led by Mao Tse-tung himself, were both unsuccessful, yet the peasant-and-labor revolutionary army formed at this time laid the nucleus of the Red Army. In the following year the Sixth National Congress of the Chinese Communist Party tardily endorsed the general principles of agrarian revolution. Mao, however, did not attend this Congress. Instead, he was actually engaged in field work in the Chingkanshan area (Hunan-Kiangsi border), where he helped build up local soviets of peasants, carry out land reform, and enlarge the Red Army. In other words, what the Party Congress outlined in empty words, Mao translated into action. When he was joined by Chu Teh, Ch'en Yi, Ho Lung, Lin Piao, and P'eng Teh-huai, he led his newly strengthened forces eastward to the Kiangsi-Fukien border and established the new soviet there with Juichin as the new seat of power (1929). This is the story in brief of the origin of the independent strength of the Communist Party as it emerged during these first crucial years of internal ferment.

In his address on "Reasons Why the Chinese Red Regime Can Survive" (October 1928), Mao stressed these factors: the characteristic structure of the rural economy of Central China, the instructive lessons of the Revolution of 1925-7, the possession of a Red Army, and the correct orientation of Communist policies. Clearly, then, from the summer of 1927 onward, there were two strains of leadership emerging in the Communist Party. The senior members were bent upon the manipulation of power and the infiltration of the Kuomintang army wherever possible. While they gave their nod to the policy of organizing the peasants, it is doubtful whether they had a clear perception of what it envisaged. Certainly, these members did nothing to carry out such a policy. On the other hand, the younger generation of leaders turned away from debates on abstract policy and went into the villages to test their program and to develop revolutionary strength in their own right. It was this development of "substantial strength" by members who had the "right idea" for steering the Revolution that enabled Mao and his close associates to become the mighty group they were in the next two decades.

Mao in subsequent years referred to this period as one of forging "the militant vanguard of the toiling masses."

"Death," said Mao, "is only the physical exit from life. And if a man, the more so a Communist, can bring some good by dying, by his brains and his courage, then he should not think twice about it. He must boldly and proudly fulfill the will of the party and the people. A party that lives for the interests of the people, which suffers with them and fights to make them happy, is an invincible force. There is no force that can conquer the party of the Communists—the militant vanguard of the toiling masses." When Mao was finally recognized by the party as its leader at the Tsung-yi conference in January 1935, it had long been an accomplished fact that his group as the group of "substantial strength" had won complete control of the party. It is perhaps an irony of history that, in striking contrast, the Kuomintang during these same years was marching in the opposite direction. Its right wing had political and military power, but no effective revolutionary program, while its left wing had an effective program but did not have substantial strength. If Wang Ching-wei, for instance, had triumphed during these early years, with strength derived not from a dependence on military men like T'ang Sheng-chih or Chang Fa-k'uei but on substantial segments of the people as a whole, subsequent events might well have pursued a different course.

In any event, with the consolidation of the Chinese Soviet Republic in Kiangsi, the program of Mao Tse-tung was vindicated. But the long struggle of the Communists against the Kuomintang had only begun. In the next twenty years the Communists overcame one difficulty after another with a single-minded determination. One of the important elements of Communist strength in this period was the development of a strong *esprit de corps* under the fires of persecution. Of the major political parties of contemporary China, the Chinese Communist Party was the youngest. When it was launched, in 1921, it had only a handful of members. From the start, the Chinese Communist Party carried one unique mark: it was suspect in the eyes of the general public. It was precisely this stigma, however, that gave the Communists their basic strength, though it slowed their growth. For while other parties, such as the Kuomintang, were quickly accepted by the public, their ranks were swollen by large numbers of opportunists with no true understanding of the party principles. The Communist Party, on the other hand, was constantly under attack. It failed to receive the old-line politicians or counterrevolutionary elements. Those who joined the party were steadfast in their zeal for the party program.

During the decade from the Nanking-Wuhan split of 1927 to the Sian incident of 1936, the Communist Party was subjected to persecution, the severity and extent of which are not yet fully understood by the outside world. No accurate statistics are available of the Communists killed during this period, but the figure certainly runs into the tens of thousands. The result of such persecution was an extraordinary sense of solidarity among the party members. The price paid in terms of human lives was tremendous, but the resultant vigor of the party was startling. The persecution helped to maintain a consistently robust stream of leadership. On account of the compactness of the surviving elements, it also helped to develop a singleness of purpose which brooked no compromise with the enemy. The dangers surrounding the party forced its members continuously to scrutinize and improve their fighting strategy. Since it was neither associated with nor exposed to the corrupting influences of the privileged groups of society, the party evolved an identity of its own. These influences combined to make it a closely knit group, small in numbers but great in strength, invincible in a qualitative rather than a quantitative sense. For instance, the iron nerve that inspired the Long March was attributable to this *esprit de corps* born of persecution. It is not too much to say that if there had not been these years of mortal peril to forge so tenacious a solidarity in the Red regime, it would have been blotted off the political map of China long ago.

While the Communist movement was threatened with persecution from outside, the triumph of the unified command achieved by the Mao Tse-tung line was continuous and unopposed from within. We have discussed the evolution of the Mao line amidst differences with Ch'en Tu-hsiu, Ch'ü Ch'iü-pai, Li Li-san, Chang Kuo-t'ao, and others. Once the validity of Mao's program was proved, however, it held control of the party without being obstructed or challenged by any effective rival program. Thus the Chinese Communist movement was spared the weakening influence of the clashes that occurred in Soviet Russia between Leninism and the leftist opposition. The main reason for this was that the economic and social conditions of China were such that the Mao line was the only effective line for the Communists to pursue. Especially important was the lack of development of the urban proletariat in China. Since the industrial workers represented an extremely small percentage of the population, a rival program championing their aspirations as against the aspirations of over three hundred million peasants was out of the question. This made the path to the achievement of a unified command in accordance with the Mao line remarkably easy. Leaders like Li Li-san who argued in favor of urban uprisings found so little support that they actually retired from positions of influence during the formative years of the Communist movement.

If solidarity and a unified command fitted the Communist machinery to lead the Revolution, the dedication to a program of mass organization sparked that machinery into militant action. The idea of "arousing the masses" certainly did not originate with the Communists. Sun Yat-sen was its greatest apostle. But it was the Communists who put teeth into the program. It was characteristic of the early Chinese Communists that they did not have the benefit of an existing political and military power that they might use. The lessons they learned in 1926 and 1927 drove home the absolute unreliability of utilizing the army of another party. When the uprisings in the summer and autumn of 1927 ended in failure, they were left with no alternative except to retreat into the remote rural areas of Kiangsi and Hunan provinces. Because they had to start from scratch, they committed themselves to a program of organizing the peasant masses. This is a point of considerable importance in understanding the undying alliance of the Communist leaders and the Chinese peasantry and in assessing the place of the Communist movement in history. The Communists were shrewd enough to recognize armed peasant rebellion as the most effective weapon in wresting the initiative of the Revolution. But their adoption of such a concrete program was as much a matter of necessity as a matter of choice. All the historian can say is that Mao and his associates were astute revolutionaries who knew where to turn to find support. It would be a mistake to attribute their adoption of the program of peasant revolution as inspired by purely idealistic motives.

Be that as it may, once they were forced to take this course by dire necessity, they put heart and soul into its pursuit. It is to their credit that they never swerved from the belief that by sticking to mass organization, they would eventually overcome all opposing forces. The classic model of mass organization adopted by the Communists was the Peasant Associations in the villages. From their inception in Hunan in 1927 till the completion of the land-reform program in 1951-2, the application of Communist strategy revolved around this formula of mass organization as the pivotal point. The vitality generated by the Peasant Associations arose from the creation of a new social order, wherein the peasants' age-long enemy, the landlords, were removed and wherein no obstacle stood in the way of the effective organization and maintenance of a strong government for the vast country-side. It may be recalled that up to this time, the control exercised by the central government virtually stopped at the hsien (county) level. From the hsien downward, the functioning of government as well as of the economy were left to the landlord class. This explains why the central government under the old regime neither enjoyed popular support nor exercised effective control of the country-side. Now, as a result of the formation of the Peasant Associations, the Communists reversed the pattern. They worked from the bottom up. They concentrated on the telling level of society, and carried out a revolution among the masses so that they not only won popular support but also secured control of the villages. The political signifi-

cance of mass organization was the primary factor that
determined the success of the Communists and the failure
of the Kuomintang.

With the new social order thus brought into being,
other measures involving mass action were carried out
with relative ease. The emancipated peasants were ready
to do the bidding of the party cadres. They were predisposed to follow their lead in setting up local self-government. They were enthusiastic in forming self-defense corps
in the villages and in volunteering for partisan warfare.
Labor teams, production co-operatives, supply auxiliaries,
and an intelligence network contributed further to the defense and economy of the Communist areas.

The greatest fruit of this aspect of the Communist
movement was, of course, the evolution of the Red Army.
Army service in China was something that heretofore had
been evaded at all costs. Although the pay in the Red Army
was low and the discipline rigorous, the peasants volun-
teered to join its ranks. The Red commanders did not
have to resort to compulsory measures in order to recruit
their men, while the fighting quality of the Communist
battalions was of a definitely superior order. There was a
sense of mission and zeal in the rank and file of the Red
Army, which could be inspired only by the implicit confidence of the men in their leaders. The spirit of comradeship, which was responsible for such a new page in Chinese
military history, was attributable to the fact that officers and men fought on a basis of equality. They were
equal in their means of livelihood, equal in the labor al-
lotted, equal in the sacrifices expected of them, and equal
in their sense of destiny. For this reason, the broad mass
base gave the Red Army an almost inexhaustible strength

in point of space and sustained it over a long period of time despite the most trying circumstances.

While the organization of the masses represented the basic trend in the development of Communist power, it was not the whole story. Mass organization explains why the Communists won. But how did they organize the masses, and how did the mass base help the Communists? The answers to these questions deserve closer examination.

In this respect, attention must be paid to the influence of the rural environment on the new order fostered by the Communists. That influence may be traced in its manifold aspects. Politically and administratively, the countryside helped the Communists to develop a spirit of honest government and public service. Since the rural economy was in a state of general poverty, participants in the Communist government had no opportunity to enrich themselves. There were no official favors that the Communist leaders could pass on to friends. The only expression of one's personality was public service and dedication to the interests of the poor. Under such circumstances, the customary phenomenon wherein government authority was based on urban concentrations of wealth and wherein officials fought for strategic positions to grab that wealth, could not repeat itself.

Furthermore, the rural areas were singularly free from foreign influence. The foreign capitalists and the Chinese comprador class clung to the urban centers. They had a strong unwillingness to go to the countryside. In their estimation, investments in the peasantry were poor risks, and working with the Communists was completely out of the question. As a consequence, this lack of contact with foreign groups had the effect of driving the Communists closer to the masses and of crystallizing an attitude of intense hostility to imperialism. The combination of ruralism with nationalism became in time an uncompromising force against the combination of urbanism with imperialism. No wonder when the Japanese invaded China they were able to recruit collaborationists from classes of people with urban affiliations, but could find few puppets among the Communists and their "partisan" supporters.

Economically China's rural population was very much underemployed. When the Communist leaders entered the field, they were struck, first of all, by the great numbers of so-called "loafers," idle and frustrated people, many well on the way to banditry. These groups were always a threat and a potential source of unrest to the Kuomintang. But the Communists turned them into a useful force. Mao Tse-tung's writings in these years show clearly the importance he attached to the problem of investing all the idle with a useful function. This would give them a cause to struggle for and a new goal for creative endeavor. As a result, the conception of a Red Army performing the dual functions of a mass army and a mass labor force was successfully implemented. The soldiers not only were taught to fight battles but were made to reclaim waste land for increased cultivation, to cut wood for shelters, and to make rudimentary weapons like hand grenades, land mines, and trench mortars. What was considered a perennial sorrow by the Kuomintang was made to contribute to the building of a great army and the improvement of the rural economy as a whole. The successful utilization of the millions of idle hands in the countryside gave the Communists the foundation upon which to base their new order.

During these years writers made much of two popular

slogans. Those writers with a city outlook delighted in saying *"T'ao t'ien chien ch'ü"* ("Go back to the farm"). Those with an eye to the villages cried *"T'ao min chien ch'ü"* ("Go among the masses"). While both slogans sounded almost alike, one reflected the complacency of city officials on the eve of retiring to their country estates, while the other pointed up the revolutionary urge to arouse the peasantry. Mao's favorite phrase in this *"T'ao min chien ch'ü"* movement was "Learn from the masses." Having turned their backs on the corruption and decadence of the government based on urban centers, those who led this movement into the countryside gradually built up a new sense of dignity and independence in the most downtrodden among the three hundred-odd million peasants. It was in the wake of this force that the Communists were able to set a premium on heroism, sacrifice, and class consciousness.

Last but not least, the importance of the Communist identification with the countryside was to be observed in their new conception of warfare. The urban centers, however strongly defended, were fixed in space and limited in number. The loss of a city meant the loss of a strategic point and was often serious in its consequences. The vast expanse of countryside presented a different story. If the Communist forces were to lose one village or one hilltop or one pass, they could always transfer their defensive operations to the next village. The losses in manpower or supplies could be kept to a negligible point. Wherever the Red forces went, they were certain to find the same economic and social conditions for the maintenance of their government and economy. No wonder the Kuomintang commanders exclaimed to their dismay: "The Red bandits emerge and disappear without rhyme or reason. Again and again they slip through our hands." This military consequence of the rural foundation of Communist power was of the utmost importance. In the Kiangsi days it was the secret of Communist survival. In the years of war with Japan it led Mao Tse-tung and Chu Teh to evolve the famous strategy that came to be known as "war of maneuver."

The keynote of Communist organization of the masses was an uncompromising boycott of all groups of privilege. The entire course of the Communist struggle for power was built upon the mass ouster of all classes of people in Chinese society whom they regarded as "feudal" or "semi-feudal." The outlawry of these classes as "the enemies of the people" was a step never attempted in past Chinese history. The Communists, however, regarded it as indispensable for the success of the Revolution.

As has been said above, Chinese society survived for two thousand years with two sharply drawn segments. The privileged minority that revolved around the monarchy and monopolized the government was responsible for nearly all the roadblocks to revolution. After every agrarian revolt they not only outlived the crisis, but invariably took the leadership away from the peasants and found their way back to new positions of power. These groups included: the military men who raised personally loyal armies to promote their own interests; the royal princes, imperial relatives, and nobles, and court eunuchs who took advantage of the Emperor's isolation from the people to abuse governmental power; the landlords whose control of the nation's wealth in the tens of thousands of villages gave them a peculiar leverage in influencing the government;

and the scholar-literati who utilized their learning to become guardians of vested interests.

For the first time in history the Communists carried out a program intended to eliminate all these groups and to seal their doom for good. To accomplish this, they drew upon the Marxist doctrine of the "dictatorship of the proletariat." But in its application to the Chinese scene, the emphasis was not so much on the elevation of the proletariat as on the permanent exclusion of certain other elements of society from the realm of public affairs. Or, to put it differently, the elevation of the proletariat was used as a weapon directed to the supreme end of overthrowing the privileged groups. The definition of the "Chinese people" set forth by the Communists after their victory in 1949 included labor, the peasantry, the petty bourgeoisie, and the national bourgeoisie as the only component parts of the "people," while the landlords, the bureaucratic capitalists, and the Kuomintang members were outlawed as "reactionaries." The Communists expected their objective to be well served by the application of this definition. Those familiar forces in history which caused the breakdown of a regime, such as the uncontrollable provincial satraps, insolent eunuchs, and imperial relatives, feudal nobles, and the intimate alliances of landlords and scholar-literati, would in their estimation be either uprooted or made powerless.

Now let us turn to the working mechanism of the Communist movement. One great source of strength for the Communists was their synchronization of reform and revolution. Throughout Chinese history, there had been reforms—in certain instances, such as under Wang An-shih of the Sung dynasty, reforms of a very far-reaching

character. Similarly, there were numerous popular revolts, many of which carried tremendous force. Thus the
Taiping Rebellion in modern times was a social upheaval
of the first magnitude. But the reforms were nearly all failures, as were most of the revolts. Where a few revolts
succeeded in establishing a new dynasty, the privileged
groups managed to assert their power, as we have noted
previously. The reason for this is not far to seek. Reforms
ordered from above could not be expected to last. Initiated
on the strength of a few forward-looking individuals but
not understood, much less supported by the people, they
could easily be killed by the privileged groups. Very often
reforms and reaction degenerated into the worst kind of
partisan fights among the privileged groups themselves.
Nor could the rebellions driven by famine and starvation
but lacking political direction prove effective. Such rebellions were variously regarded as banditry or insurrection,
depending upon the scale of the eruption. But in either
case they spent their force in short order, for they represented military adventure in a primitive form. Wang An-
shih and Hung Hsiu-chuan were men of no lesser ambition than Mao Tse-tung; but their mistake was failure to
integrate reform and revolt.

The Communists struck a new path. They carried out
agricultural reforms at the same time that they were raising a revolutionary army. The reforms took root because
they met the urgent needs of the peasants in the villages.
These reforms yielded tangible benefits to the masses and
were jealously guarded by them. The operation of this
process facilitated the raising of the Red Army. From
the days when the peasants fought with their pitchforks
and sickles till the time when the full-fledged army was

equipped with modern arms, one distinguishing mark of the Communist army was that it represented no isolated military venture but the military phase of a social revolution. This interweaving of measures of reform and revolution presented a spectacle never witnessed before in Chinese history. Thus a typical Communist movement in a Chinese village embraced these successive stages: formation of Peasant Associations; organization of armed bands; spread of uprisings incited by hunger; refusal to pay taxes and rents; petitions and demands listing popular needs; confiscation of grain and other property of the rich; aggregation of greater numbers of followers; formation of soviets or establishment of new regimes under Communist direction. In this intricate maze of action it was impossible to separate reform and revolution from one another.

The welding of political and military power into one indivisible whole was perhaps inevitable under the given circumstances. With the persecution by the Kuomintang, the Communist movement could not have survived if it had failed to improvise means for self-defense. Yet the formulation of policies with the calculated objective of making reform and revolution complement one another was certainly no accident. In this connection, the Liang-shan-po tradition, *"t'i t'ien hsing tao chiu sheng min"* ("carry out the Way of Heaven in order to save the people"), immortally embodied in the *Shui Hu Chuan (All Men Are Brothers)* exerted a great influence on the Communist leaders. The heroes depicted in this popular novel championed the cause of the poor and expropriated the property of the wealthy. They made it their job to defy the established authority. Organization of the oppressed masses into armed units, employment of rough justice, and the use of mobile bands in inter-village raids were among the commonest occurrences in this romance. Last but not least, the sanctity of the bond of bandit brotherhood and a general fearlessness of spirit were qualities held in high esteem. These elements, as is evident, thoroughly combined the economic demands of the people with direct military action. While it may be excessive to allege, as some observers do, that Mao Tse-tung finds special satisfaction in viewing himself as a latter-day reincarnation of some of these heroes, yet it is clear that the Communists owe their spiritual descent to this tradition more than to anything else in so far as their revolutionary strategy is concerned.

The Communists not only succeeded in integrating their political and military power, but in the new ferment the Red Army emerged as infinitely superior to other armies familiar in Chinese history. The main reason was that the Red Army was an army of the people, while the armies under the old regimes comprised mercenaries in the hire of the privileged groups. The development of the Red Army reflected whatever good traditions of army-raising were to be found in Chinese history. Thus it retained certain features of *Fu-pin* (the farmer-soldier draft system of the Northern Dynasties and early T'ang) ; of *T'un-t'ien* (military colonization practiced under the Han and several subsequent dynasties) ; and *Min-t'uan* (local militia of the Ming and Ch'ing dynasties) . But it surpassed them all by virtue of its identification with the interests of the people. For the first time in Chinese history, the army was not a predatory weapon employed against the people, but an instrument used to remove social abuses for the people.

For the first time the army was not a congregation of bandits in disguise, but a true medium of national policy.

A word must be said in this connection about guerrilla warfare. The guerrillas served as a support for the regular Red Army. The fundamental concept of guerrilla warfare was total mobilization to turn every village into a fighting base. The human factor, the willing co-operation of the entire population of the countryside, was the key to such mobilization. Emphasis was not placed on large-scale battles with the enemy; it was centered rather on sporadic and desultory engagements such as were within the capacity of the peasant fighters. Furthermore, since the guerrilla bands were peasants in arms, they did not seek a quick decision on the battlefield, but were quite prepared for a prolonged struggle in order to wear out the enemy. The objective was to win victory over a superior enemy by attrition and by preserving themselves. The resort to sabotage, especially in supplies and by means of intelligence, was another potent arm of guerrilla warfare. All in all, if there had been no guerrilla fighting, it is doubtful whether the Red Army alone could have scored its many outstanding victories. It is not without interest that in the Kuomintang-controlled areas during the war with Japan, the nonexistence of guerrillas made it virtually impossible for the Kuomintang army to penetrate behind the enemy lines.

It may be recalled that in 1926–7, when the Communists had to rely upon certain sympathetic units in the Kuomintang army to further their political program, they suffered one defeat after another. Once they had built up their own armed strength, however, the power and prestige of the Red Army grew rapidly. First, as no party could wield any power without an army, especially when its opposition was directed against the Kuomintang, the Communist Party with its own Red Army soon attracted to its banners the National Salvationists, the Democratic League, and other liberal and leftist groups. These groups, unable to hold their own ground, were forced by circumstances to co-operate with the Communists. Moreover, after the Red Army had achieved a reasonably impressive record, it developed a great ability to induce desertions among the Kuomintang forces. A subtle interplay of the corroding influence of Communist ideas, the threat of annihilation, and the attractive offer of humane treatment following defection resulted in many instances of Kuomintang desertions. During the Kiangsi period, large numbers of troops under General Chu Pei-teh went over to the Reds, while in the famous third anti-Communist campaign the troops under the command of General Sun Lien-chung staged the sensational Ningtu uprising, which gave the Reds the nucleus of their future Fifth Army.

There is still another aspect of the Red Army which is of overriding importance. From the standpoint of state finance, the Red Army was not a strain on the Communist treasury as were the armies of the Kuomintang and other previous regimes on their treasuries. During the decade 1928–37 about seventy-five per cent of the Kuomintang budget was consumed by military expenditures. The Communists did not have such a huge financial burden. The peasants, rewarded by social reforms rather than by pay, joined the Red Army to render service. They took care of their subsistence by their own means of production. There was no huge military budget for the Communist treasury to carry, and the Red Army fought with excellent morale. Under these circumstances, it became unnecessary for the Communist government to levy all kinds of exactions in cash or in kind upon the peasants, as was the case in Kuomintang-controlled areas. This is the basic reason why, in spite of tremendous odds, the Red Army survived and grew.

In this dramatic spectacle of supporting reform with a revolutionary army, the Communists relied heavily on the skillful use of Communist ideology. The question is often raised how Marxism-Leninism could have been applied with such telling effect in China, in view of the vast differences in historical and sociological background between China and Russia. Before answering the question, one must of course remember that up to the present stage the application of Marxism-Leninism to the Chinese Revolution by Mao and his colleagues has been highly selective. The Mao Tse-tung line has been a revised version of the parent Communist ideology, made to suit China's peculiar conditions. Thus, Mao insisted on the use of the peasantry as the base for the Chinese Revolution. He further took the position that the Chinese Revolution would have to go through a transitional stage of the "joint dictatorship of several revolutionary classes" before conditions could be created for the Revolution to march toward its ultimate goal of socialism.

For these shifts Mao had been criticized for "deviation" or "heresy." It is doubtful, however, whether such charges ever weighed heavily with him. He not only violated the dogma of the parent ideology but treated its defenders with a surprising casualness until they turned around to bless him with their belated approval. Moreover, Mao's thinking was probably just the reverse of that of his critics. In his estimation, the so-called "deviation" was precisely the step necessary to prepare and fortify the Communist ideology for effective application in China. At all stages Mao insisted that the leadership of the Chinese Revolution belonged to the proletariat. It was only because the proletariat was not well developed while the peasantry represented the bulk of the oppressed classes that Mao advocated the peasant base and the joint dictatorship of several revolutionary classes. In Mao's mind, then, a preliminary deviation was justified in view of his determination to conform in the end. In fact, Mao seems to have implied that he had to deviate before he could hope to conform. The academic discussion of Mao's deviation, therefore, should not be carried too far. Although the question of how long deviation will last has been left unanswered, it is important to realize that the Chinese Communists have at no time divorced themselves from long-range ties with Marxism-Leninism and that, time and again, they have affirmed their implicit loyalty to that parent ideology. There is a saying in China which applies with particular cogency in this instance: *"Yi t'u t'ung kuei"* ("Different itineraries; same destination").

Having explained how Mao's revisions sought to fit the Communist ideology to the existing realities of the Chinese Revolution, one can account for the effectiveness of this alien philosophy in China in a variety of ways. For one thing, the Communists, in carrying out their radical reforms, were anxious to seek the freedom of action which an alien and little-understood ideology alone could make possible. It was precisely the total strangeness of the Communist creed that made it so useful to the Chinese Communist leaders. As far as the masses of the Chinese people were concerned, they did not comprehend in any event what the Red theoreticians propounded. The Red leaders, however, found in the body of Communist ideology a ready answer to any argument set forth by their opponents. This strange ideology, with its facile rationale, was therefore a convenient and effective weapon for silencing opposition— a blockbuster, as it were, against all the traditional attitudes and values.

The Chinese found the Communist doctrine a most potent weapon for the task of destroying the resistance of the privileged groups. This ideology, pointing to the inevitable war between the proletariat and the capitalists, lent poignancy to the struggle between the landless and the landlords. In the revolutionary march of the landless it forced the landlords to surrender, for in the Communist calculus they were the counterrevolutionary force. It is interesting to recall that none of the peasant revolts in past history ever had so mighty an argument. They took on the protection of certain religious cults, which were mystic enough to rouse the peasants to action but not powerful enough to overcome opposition. The Communist ideology was a clear and unequivocal bid for a new social order. For the peasants, it was clearly a program which met their needs and for which they would fight. For the privileged groups, it denoted a moral sentence that they found hard to refute.

It has been characteristic of the Communist strategy to put forth theories a step or two beyond the people's actual comprehension of the Marxist-Leninist dogma. As far as the victims of the Revolution (the landlords and other privileged groups) were concerned, such a propaganda offensive created a mental and psychological storm that disarmed resistance and induced submission. As far as the

followers of the Revolution (the masses) were concerned,
it inspired a vague belief that the next step would always
be better than the present. To rely thus on the great reper-
tory of Marxist-Leninist doctrine was a paying proposition.
In all this, of course, Communist China followed the path
of Soviet Russia. The very fact that Soviet Russia was successful and that China proceeded to cement close relations
with world Communism lent further strength to this strategy.

In yet another sense, the play of the Communist ideology has been of infinite value to the Chinese Communists.
The determinism in the Communist philosophy—the doctrine that there exists a predeterminable course of history
pointing to the redemption of the poor and the oppressed,
and that the Communist leaders as the elite hold the key
to this course—put the Red leaders on Olympian heights
in wielding their revolutionary power. This Marxian determinism fitted in well with the temperament of the Chinese people, who were inured to a fatalistic outlook upon
life. Right or wrong, the decisions and actions of the
Communist leaders became immune to any questioning or
criticism, in the same manner as the divine right of kings
placed the conduct of the emperors in past ages beyond all
criticism. Like the Chinese emperor, who as the Son of
Heaven knew the correct will of Heaven, the Red leaders
as followers of Marx and Lenin stood on the implicit claim
that they knew the inexorable direction which history
would take. This over-all assumption not only divested the
Communists of the fetters of tradition and social conven-
tion, but gave them a free hand in directing their activities,
without being held responsible to the opinions of others.

This brief appraisal of the application of the Communist ideology to the Chinese Revolution will not be complete without repeating once more the basic internal strength that the Communists have built up themselves. However militant the ideas of Communism may have been in furthering their tasks, they have been borrowed to provide extra vigor to an inner solidarity that the Communist leaders had already achieved among themselves. Otherwise the course of events might well have been very different. At the time of the 1924 reorganization of the Kuomintang, Sun Yat-sen took Russian advice and direction and imposed them on a loose Kuomintang membership. As the Kuomintang was inherently weak, the application of the Russian technique and ideology resulted in hopeless dissension. No new vigor was generated; much vitality was lost. Mao Tse-tung and his associates started off with the building of internal strength and solidarity. There was no dissension. Under such circumstances, the borrowing of Marxist-Leninist ideology, even though foreign and full of discrepancies, resulted in adding new power to a base that was already unassailable.

In view of what has been said in the foregoing paragraphs, it is clear that the Communists have built up the major part of their strength in their own right. But one must not forget that propaganda as a weapon used during the entire period of subversion contributed considerably to the power of the Communists. Reference has been made to the familiar tactics of infiltrating the Kuomintang ranks and to the corroding influence of Communist ideas. Even more potent was that peculiar aspect of propaganda which may be called accusation by half-truths. During the Kiangsi days, the Communist propaganda machine painted such a black picture of the "feudalistic exploitation of the

masses" by the Kuomintang that it was tantamount to taking advantage of the people's ignorance in its suppression
of all the facts about economic reconstruction under the
ægis of the Nanking government. The Communists accused Nanking of levying 1,700 kinds of taxes but they
failed to mention the fact that there had been about 3,000
kinds of taxes when the Kuomintang assumed control. In
April 1932 Juichin made a formal declaration of war
against Japan. This was little more than a gesture to extort political advantage. It was common knowledge that
hostilities would hardly break out between the Japanese
in Manchuria or Shanghai and the Chinese Communists
in the mountain fastnesses of Kiangsi and Hunan.

One must also recall that throughout the period of the
Tangku truce and the Ho-Umetsu agreement in the early
1930's, the Communists incessantly accused Nanking of
secret undertakings to recognize the puppet state of "Manchukuo." This did much harm to the position of the Nanking government, as was evidenced in the wavering of
many industrial and business leaders, the rise of the National Salvationists, and the Student Movement of December 1935. Yet, in the Chang-Kawagoe negotiations in
September–December 1936, the Nanking government stub-
bornly resisted the Japanese demands. The declarations of
General Chiang at Kuling prior to the outbreak of the war
further proved his readiness to face the Japanese threat.
But the Communist propaganda had already created such
an unfavorable impression of Chiang that it alone remained in the minds of the people.

Throughout their twenty years of struggle with the
Kuomintang, the Communists proved their astuteness in
master-minding every situation. They seldom hesitated to

sacrifice the consistency of their policy for the sake of survival or of winning an advantage. Expedience in the choice of methods was surpassed only by the singleness of purpose in their struggle for power. It seemed that no situation was too hard to be resolved; no opportunity, however slim, escaped their notice without being exploited to its full advantage. Through an alternation of patience and boldness, of pretense and propaganda, they managed to wrest initiative and victory from their enemy. If ever there was a case wherein the leaders of revolution may be said to have triumphed by the very strength of a creative imagination, that may well be affirmed about the Communists of China.

It must not be thought, however, that in their ambition for power the Communists neglected to devise safety valves for venting possible popular dissatisfaction. In this connection, the Communist leaders were alive to the need of avoiding the isolation of the government from the people. After all, in exploiting the new power generated by mass organization, the Communist leaders stood in the same position as the ruling classes of the new dynasties in the past. Accordingly, they turned their attention to the problem of retaining their monopoly of power while avoiding isolation from the masses. It was this isolation that in past ages inevitably brought about the decay and fall of the government. The Communist solution was to maintain a semblance of wide popular participation in government.

From the very beginning of the struggle, the Communists made it a basic point in their program to bring more and more people into local government. The famous three-thirds system, followed in administrations in Communist areas during the war (with the Communists, the

Kuomintang, and non-party members each forming one third of the administration), was one illustration of the Communist technique in building up a seeming mass participation in government. Another cornerstone of Communist policy was the plan to draw an increasing number of people into all manner of political meetings, study groups, public rallies, parades, and demonstrations. These measures carried little substantial meaning as far as genuine popular control of the government was concerned. While the groups thus assembled were largely non-Communist, the power to make and determine policy was tightly held in the hands of the top leadership of the party. But they did bridge the gap between the government and the people. By detecting popular grievances, precluding the rise of opposition, and forestalling the demand for genuine democratic rights, these gatherings succeeded in orientating the education of the masses as the Communists desired.

As long as the Communists in control were capable of securing to the people a reasonable degree of welfare, these superficial measures had the salutary effect of keeping their government anchored in the contented hearts of the masses. Here again the economic underdevelopment and the slow growth of mass political consciousness were the greatest assets for the Communist leaders. Largely on account of these factors, they succeeded in avoiding the dangers of being isolated from the people. Perhaps in more advanced countries such spurious expedients would have been assessed at their true value. But in China this policy of encouraging apparent popular participation in government, hypocritical as it was, paid great dividends to the Communists.

In any discussion of Communist strength and success, due consideration must be given to two more factors: namely, the importance of the war with Japan in the spread of Communist power, and the quick termination of the civil war, bringing with it the restoration of peace.

The importance to the Communists of the war with Japan was twofold. For one thing, as we have seen, it forced the Kuomintang to expend its major military resources in the struggle with the external foe, and thus reduced the Kuomintang to the position of a regional regime. To Lukouchiao the Communists owed their godsent opportunity to extend their control over North China and thenceforth to seize total power. In still another sense, the war with Japan was vital to the success of the Communists. It is characteristic of a sedate agricultural society like that of China that unless there is a great upheaval such as that caused by war or invasion with its mass migrations of population, it is virtually impossible to carry out any sweeping social reforms. The fact that the *Chün T'ien* system could be carried out following the disunion and civil war in pre-T'ang periods, while it failed in periods of peace and stability, is a good historical illustration. It is true that Communist reforms in Kiangsi were carried out in the early 1930's. But it is equally true that by 1935 they were wiped out by the reaction. In Yenan, on the eve of war with Japan, the Communists' attempt to resume their program was attended with insurmountable difficulties. The coming of the war removed the inertia of the sedate society. It loosened its roots, broke down the time-honored conventions and inhibitions, dislocated the economic and population structure, and set new values and a new outlook in men's minds. It caused such a change

throughout the land that it simplified most of the tasks
confronting the Communists and enabled them to expand
their organization and control throughout the villages of
North China. In this process the mass slaughter and destruction wrought by the Japanese and the scorched-earth
policy of the Chinese defenders alike contributed to the
success of the Communists. Following the great dislocations of the war, there could be no return to the old ways.
As the people looked for the dawn of a new day, the
golden opportunity for the Communists arrived. Had there
not been the war and had the population and social structure remained unshaken, it is almost certain that the Communists would not have achieved so speedy a victory.

By V–J Day the destiny of China had no doubt already
been decided in favor of the Communists. Their strength
was too deeply rooted over too great an area to be dislodged by the Kuomintang. Yet the great civil war that was
just unfolding could well have developed into a long-
drawn-out affair and sapped the nascent power of the
Communists. The Kuomintang forces were well equipped,
and their numbers were certainly not inferior. Moreover,
the political and military groups of the Kuomintang realized that, once defeated, they would find no hospitable
quarters under the Communist regime. The Kuomintang
expected that even if they did not gain victories, the government would be able to hold the Red Army in a prolonged stalemate. Such a situation would repeat the history of past epochs when loyalist armies of a fallen dynasty
succeeded in holding certain key provinces and in pro-
longing their opposition to the new regime. At times it
required one or two decades before these remnants of
resistance were completely suppressed. To say the least,

a prolonged civil war would seriously have endangered the Red Army. Worse still, a stalemate could well have led to a wavering of public morale, which in turn would have afforded time for the Kuomintang to organize a counter-attack. Speedy victory was the *sine qua non* of complete Communist success. Moreover, time was of the essence for the achievement of peace and unification. The more speedily civil government was restored and hostilities ended, the simpler and surer would be the task of achieving recovery and good administration. It is not too much to say that if the Communists had not defeated the Kuomintang in blitzkrieg fashion, or if the civil war had had to be drawn out for a number of years, they might not have been able to win a conclusive victory over the Kuomintang.

The fact that the Communists were able to achieve so swift a victory is viewed by certain quarters as a near miracle. The truth of the matter is that they won on two counts. For one thing, they did not act with haste in the battlefield. The strategists took time to plan their moves. As a result, they did not have to decimate every Kuomintang division but rather compelled most of them to desert or surrender. There was no seesaw battle; the Red legions rolled on from one major theater to another in rapid succession. Whatever battles they fought struck at the vital perimeters of Kuomintang defense so that isolated pockets of resistance could have little meaning. Another reason for the speedy victory of the Communists—and this is even more significant than the former—was the loss by the Kuomintang of the support of the village gentry and city merchants. The economic deterioration and government fumbling from 1947 onward were such that a general atmosphere of despair enveloped the classes which were the customary pillars of the Kuomintang government. The Kuomintang forces had to join battle with the enemy like lone battalions, denied the support of the groups of which they were the avowed champions. This was a direct reversal of the situation created in the years of the Taiping Rebellion, just about a century ago. The times, both then and now, were periods of great storm and stress. Both actions were centered in the trans-Yangtze regions. But while Tseng Kuo-fan could create fresh units of *"hsiang-yung"* ("village braves") to fight the Taiping rebels because he had the solid support of the gentry, General Chiang Kai-shek in 1947–9 found it hard to rally the gentry to his cause. For twenty years Chiang had stood for the landlord and the privileged classes; but in this hour of need, they failed to respond to his call. Such was the futility of his policy that he had to throw the Kuomintang army, otherwise magnificently supplied and equipped, into what was obviously a lost struggle. The victory of the Communists was thus in the last analysis due to the prostration of the Kuomintang brought on by the falling away of its habitual sources of support.

III

THE CHARACTER AND MOOD
OF THE NEW REGIME

❀

THE CULMINATION of the economic and social revolution under Communist leadership has brought China to the threshold of a new age of unification and strength. Unlike the Bolshevik Revolution in Russia, the Communist accession to power has been followed by a fast recovery and the remarkably smooth establishment of a strong central government. Many of its measures, both internal and external, are widely deplored and condemned. But a comparison of the degree of chaos and turmoil prior to 1949 and the stability so quickly achieved since then makes the Peking government a source of amazement to the world. The ubiquitous question is: how could they do it? This new regime has been a veritable prodigy, performing under the influence of men not unfamiliar, yet strange, and along paths not unheard of, yet defying the beliefs of its contemporaries. The regime is reminiscent of the power of some of the great dynasties in China's past, and yet it strikes radical departures from the old ways of empire-building. For a true understanding of the character and mood of the new regime, we need to consider some of its salient features and trends.

The most powerful factor which has enabled the Peking regime to set a distinctive tone for the new era is that it has brought both peace and unification to the people. The importance of these factors in a country like China with its teeming population living close to a subsistence level cannot be overstated. Any regime that holds the key to either of the two blessings has a good chance of winning the people. Whatever group achieves both will no doubt control the country. For peace provides the background for recovery, while unification ensures the necessary conditions for effective government. For almost half a century, with one group after another fighting for control, the Chinese people have not enjoyed either of the two. But now the scourge of civil war has come to an end. When the Communists took over in 1949, their victory was more complete than was generally believed at the time. Not only did many of the Kuomintang divisions surrender, but the remnants of the defeated army failed to attempt a comeback. The usual phenomena of regional opposition maintained by warlords surviving the change of regimes have not repeated themselves. This has prevented much bloodshed and expedited the work of rehabilitation. In fact, the unification of the country was so thorough that even distant Tibet was speedily brought under the control of the Peking government.

Meantime, the danger of foreign intervention no longer exists. The two chief reasons for foreign intervention in the past—imperialist powers bent on a "divide and rule" policy and warring factions inside China working in league with such foreign powers—have been effectively ruled out. Japan is no longer a threat to Chinese unity. The Western imperialist powers have been removed from the Chinese scene as a result of World War II. There are no recalcitrant warlords inside the country who would be the willing tools of the imperialists. From the standpoint of external danger, then, the Communist regime also finds itself confronting no enemy. (Communist propaganda, of course, deliberately depicts the United States as the new imperialist enemy of China, a view that is not warranted by facts. The motives behind this allegation will be discussed in a subsequent chapter.) This has made the position of the Peking government since 1949 vastly different from that of the Soviet government after 1918. Russia in the decade of 1918–28 faced civil and economic deterioration as well as foreign intervention. The Bolshevik Revolution ushered in, as it were, all sorts of troubles, and the Soviet government was not stabilized until about 1928. The Chinese Communists, on the other hand, had their years of ordeal prior to 1949. Their troubles were resolved during the period of insurrection, with the result that the victory of 1949 marked the dawn of peace and unification.

What did this mean to the Communist regime? The achievement of peace and unification meant that the new government could begin its work from strength. For the first time in many decades, even generations, the people saw the way clear to a new dedication of their lives. The extensive devastations of the war constituted no marked hindrance because the outlook was hopeful. The native industriousness of the people, hampered so long by insecurity and chaos, could now proceed with new energy. It is an interesting commentary on the pulse of the new age that production indices which during the civil war showed a thirty per cent drop below the peak figure of prewar years not only regained normalcy but registered a fifteen per cent increase over that figure in 1952. Under these conditions the new government has rapidly accumulated strength. This is perhaps the basic explanation of the strong sense of confidence among the leaders of Peking. The people, enjoying a peaceful recovery, are predisposed to yield to their rule and overlook some of their faults.

The leaders in Peking are exultant and self-assured. They are keenly aware of their mission, and they are determined to utilize whatever talent and vision they possess. In the parlance of the Chinese historical scholar, these men would be called *"p'u yi chiang hsiang"* ("denim-shirt generals and prime ministers") . They have risen from the ranks of the common man and have no aristocratic affiliations. They have a shrewd understanding of the problems and needs of the masses. Above all, they have a great ambition for power. In a very real sense, their prototypes were the founders of the Han dynasty; in fact, the term *"p'u yi chiang hsiang"* comes from the annals of that dynasty. If one were to place Mao Tse-tung, Chu Teh, Chou En-lai, P'eng Teh-huai alongside the names of Liu Pang, Hsiao Ho, Fan Kuan, and Kuan Yin, the similarities in their sociological and psychological backgrounds and in their pattern of action would indeed seem striking. Like the Han founders, they are plebeian stalwarts exploiting a mass revolutionary upsurge for the seizure of power. Just as the Han founders overthrew the descendants of the old ruling families of the Six States who were the residual nobility of the feudal age, so have the Communists overthrown the influential social groups under the Kuomintang. Both represent the rise to power of the humble, people never dignified with any social standing prior to victory in their struggle.

One thing, however, differentiates the Communist lead-

ers from the Han founders. The leaders of the Han dynasty
quickly enlisted the services of the landlord-scholar class
and relied upon Confucianism as an instrument of government. The power they seized was not only shared with the
landlord-scholars, but in time actually passed into the
hands of the latter. The current situation with the Communist leaders is vastly different. As we have seen in the
preceding chapters, the concentration of power in the top
level of the Communist leadership is tight. These new
leaders of China are determined to keep power in the
hands of their own group and refuse to enlist the services
of other classes of people. They—and they alone—will
exercise the power of ruling the new state. It is interesting to recall that at the time when the original Han leadership was losing ground to the Confucian scholars, Emperor
Wen Ti lamented to his imperial household that the landlord-scholar class and their Confucianism were "the deadly
force that will end our dynasty." As though heeding this
warning, the Communists today are determined not to
allow their leadership to go by default as it did under the
Han dynasty.

What is happening, then, is that there is a new alignment of social classes in government. Under the old pattern, the alignment was the monarchy plus the landlord-
scholar class against the peasantry. When the peasants
revolted, they often succeeded in upsetting the monarchy,
but they almost always lost their leadership to the landlord-
scholar class, who would in turn line up with the new monarchy to oppress the peasantry. Now, for the first time, a
new force has emerged to champion the cause of the peasants, but the rest of the process is not to be repeated. Not
only have they overthrown the equivalent of the monarchy,

but they have liquidated the landlord-scholar class, so that the usual spectacle of the latter usurping the leadership and transferring it to a new monarchy cannot occur. Instead, the new force (that is, the Communist Party) has kept the leadership for itself. In other words, between the governing and the governed, there is no longer an intervening class. The Communists deal directly with the peasant masses, with no brokers, as it were, between them. The future development of China thus will differ radically from the development of the Han or other dynasties. There exists no force that can dilute the control exercised by the Communists. This is why the Communist leaders of China practice no tolerance and make no compromises with other groups. They are determined to make themselves masters of the new China.

In eliminating the landlord-scholar class to ensure their own monopoly of power, however, the Communist leaders have made a mockery of their plebeian stand. The government in Peking today is neither a government of nor for nor by the people. The Communists have capitalized on the revolutionary forces unleashed in the upsurge of the masses and seized power for themselves. In truth, the peasantry is no better protected today under the Communist regime than it was under the Han or in other periods. But as the Communists do not permit or delegate another social class to rule over the peasants, the entire face of Chinese society has changed its complexion. The directness of their association with the masses and the strict monopoly of power make it impossible for anyone to challenge their alleged identification with the interests of the masses. As a result, the Communists have no difficulty in claiming to be their spokesmen. Mao argues: "As there is no political party in China representing exclusively the peasant class, and as political parties representing the liberal bourgeoisie lack a resolute agrarian policy, the Chinese Communists, who have a firm land program and who really fight for the interests of the peasants, securing the broad mass as their allies, as a result have become the leaders of the peasants and all revolutionary democrats. . . ." These words, plausible as they are, still cannot conceal the fact that the Communist rule is a pseudo-plebeian regime actually imposed on the masses. Here, evidently, the traditional attitude of the Chinese that government is an affair for the elite is of invaluable help to the Communist dictatorship. The doctrine *"pu tsai ch'i wei, pu mou ch'i shih"* ("people who are not in seats of power should not interfere with the government") is the real instrument that has enabled the Communists to pose as the champions of the masses. The Communists, in disowning the landlord-scholars, have themselves stepped into the landlord-scholar role of being the repository of all governmental wisdom and skill.

How can the Communists carry off such autocracy and dictatorship? In this connection, there are certain qualities in the Communist leaders that deserve consideration. The Communist leaders are seasoned in field work and rich in practical experience. The old-style literati or armchair officials are not found among them. Ever since Mao left the Route Vallon (Shanghai) office in his dramatic protest against Kuomintang ineptitude, his life has for the most part been spent in the villages, dedicated to the good earth, toiling and fighting together with the hungry and destitute masses. This has given him a penetrating insight into China's economy and the concrete problems of the Revolution. The same is true of his colleagues. Almost none of the Communist leaders of today were good students in the conventional sense of the term. *"Lo p'o kiang hu"* ("roving about rivers and lakes in reduced circumstances") was the fit description of these men in their adolescent life. But their disdain for cloistered scholarship was matched by a lively vision, a bouyant frame of mind, an eagerness for action, and, above all, a capacity for hard work. It is these traits that give the Communist leaders a special qualification for nation-building today.

Looking back in history, in any epoch of greatness the leading statesmen were as a rule well-versed in both civil administration and warfare, in economic planning and frontier affairs, in letters and in farming. The Communist leaders, too, are men of practical experience and earthy common sense. Their intimate association with the problems of the people, their ability to fit theories to realities, plus their willingness to undergo all manner of physical hardship, form the pillars of their strength today. Marxist-Leninist teachings may have sparked certain lines of revolutionary thinking in the Communist leaders, but all in all their field work and field experience have made them the tough fighters that they are. At one stage in the Communists' prolonged struggle against the Kuomintang army, the Red commanders were shown the political and military catechism of Stalin, which was reputed to be a masterly formula for victory. Upon perusing the piece, the Chinese Red officers exclaimed that had they followed such a plan, their men would have been annihilated long ago. The Chinese Communists were gratified that they had worked out their own plans in accordance with the given circumstances.

A word of comparison of Mao Tse-tung, Sun Yat-sen, and General Chiang Kai-shek is perhaps of interest. There is no doubt that Sun was a great revolutionary thinker, but he was not a field worker. Both Mao and Chiang, however, are men of action. Both are revolutionary workers rather than visionaries, fighters rather than teachers. It was characteristic of Sun that he poured forth a stream of great revolutionary ideas, not unlike a philosopher meditating in his ivory tower; but he often lost control of a situation when it came to practical execution. Mao and Chiang, on the other hand, are organizers of the first order. Their struggle for power has frequently been heightened by a vindictiveness toward the opponent. Mao's triumph over Chiang was due to the fact that he marched with the forces of revolution while Chiang marched against them. The verdict of the future historian will probably declare that Sun prophesied the Revolution, Chiang tried it, but Mao, in his own fashion, did the work needed to consummate it.

In the circle of Peking's leaders today, Mao Tse-tung has been elevated to extraordinary heights of prestige. But an idolatrous worship of him has not occurred. Mao's leadership continues to be a creative force, in the sense that it leads the nation to newer and greater endeavors. Back in the 1920's, following the death of Sun Yat-sen, the Kuomintang immediately canonized the dead leader. This stultified adoration of the leader, making everything he said and did infallible, is perhaps the most unfortunate thing that can happen to a revolutionary movement. To say the least, deification or canonization is the precursor of hypocrisy. Worse still, it can cause a stagnation of spirit by making everything empty and sterile. It is to the credit of the Chinese Communists that such a movement has not taken place with regard to Mao. To be sure, there is unceasing praise of Mao, of his policies and accomplishments. But on more than one occasion, Mao has himself led movements to curb those very tendencies among party members which threatened to degenerate into a blind and unthinking worship of him and his principles. Mao puts dogmatism, subjectivity, and formalism as among the worst evils that should be stamped out among his followers. In any event, along with Mao's increasing prestige, the new regime has continuously been moving ahead. This has made Mao a rallying center for further constructive effort rather than the occasion for idle applause. Regardless of the merits of their policies, Mao and his associates appear to retain all the vigor of a forward movement rather than of one that has already spent itself. Mao has not come to be regarded as a superhuman entity, but remains the effective leader he was before. For that reason the Communist regime has grown into a powerful going concern for national rejuvenation.

This basic humanism in the Communist leadership is at once the cause and effect of the small world of democratic practice which exists within the top echelons of the Peking oligarchy. In this respect the Politburo of the Chinese Communist Party is different from its counterpart in the Russian Communist Party. There is little sense of humor in the operation of the Russian Politburo, whereas the Chinese Politburo has an abundance of it. In this sense, the leaders of Peking are very Chinese indeed. Mao does not "high-hat" his associates. He consults them. He does not overrule his colleagues by raw methods, but seeks to unify them by common consent. Most of his decisions are reached after discussions with his colleagues, and they represent a collective judgment. Such harmonious comradeship is not at all accidental: it was born of years of hard struggle. Understanding as Mao does the dangerous consequences of internal dissension after so many years of bitter struggle, he spares no pains in fostering the cohesion of the team around him. One of the reasons for his gradual withdrawal from public functions in recent years is his assumption of an increasing measure of responsibility in weaving his official family into a harmonious whole. It is for this reason that power is highly concentrated at the top of the Chinese Communist Party, and yet the whole government apparatus in Peking works with remarkable smoothness. What makes the giant dictatorship tick is the democratic spirit at the top of the regime.

This does not mean that the Chinese Communist leaders are naturally endowed with greater wisdom or greater capacity for harmonious teamwork. Mao's ingenuity in maintaining a strong sense of brotherhood among his associates seems to depend on three factors. First, he does not surround himself with a coterie of servile supporters to advance his own power over that of the others. Second, as the growth of the Communist movement creates constantly expanding vistas of new revolutionary tasks, Mao makes it a point to assign added responsibilities to his colleagues, thereby stimulating them to spread their efforts farther afield rather than to consume themselves with internal quarrels. Third, Mao understands the temperament of the Chinese too well to attempt the role of a Führer. The Chinese people are more rational than religious. Instead of submitting to a demigod, Mao's colleagues are more prepared to support him as the senior member in a company of equals. This strategy is perhaps the most important focal point in the inner workings of the Communist leadership.

Other revolutionary groups, such as the Kuomintang, and the Bolsheviks of Russia, have also experienced great hardship. But the trend there has been toward one-man dictatorship. When power resides in one man, then cliques arise, each pledging allegiance to the dictator, but none loyal to the state. The overeagerness to concentrate power in these instances often defeats its own purpose. It has at times caused the downfall of the entire movement, or has led to endless conspiracies of one leader against another. Peking seems to have achieved a different scheme for stabilizing the oligarchy. The remarkable harmony within the Politburo enables it to govern with a safe and competent hand. The removal of Li Li-san as chairman of the All-China Federation of Trade Unions, of Po Yi-po as Minister of Finance, of General Yeh Chien-ying as Mayor of Canton, and the demise of Kao Kang of Manchuria— these are essentially different from the purges in Soviet Russia because they have been carried out without any peril to the prestige of the government. When, for instance, Beria was removed by Malenkov, the repercussions shook the entire edifice of Soviet rule. Such purges serve to bring forth the inherent weakness of a despotic government. The Peking Politburo has shown no fear or misgivings in removing undesirable officials. The dismissals or demotions have not been accompanied by any signs of danger. As the actions of the Politburo are not tarnished by ulterior motives, its internal unity remains intact.

The character of the Communist leadership has been

discussed at some length because it has a direct bearing on the future. The leaders in Peking today are for the most part in their sixties. Will their successors be able to carry on the same type of leadership? The view generally advanced is that, unlike the founders of the Communist movement, the new leaders will not have the hardships of the early years to bind them together in a strong solidarity. This view is quite true, but only up to a certain point. The challenge of the era of reconstruction, with its stupendous problems, can be as great as the challenge presented in the period of subversion, if not greater. The determining factors in the success or failure of the new generation of leaders are to be sought elsewhere. Most important of all, if Mao's successor continues his policy of discouraging personal cliques, then the battle will largely be won by him. Next in importance, he needs imagination and tolerance. It is imagination that has given Mao his breadth of vision and flexibility of policy, that has made him alive to the realities without turning pedantic or doctrinaire. As for tolerance, it is another great gift that his successors can ill afford to ignore. Tolerance wins support through consent, a source of strength which any leader, especially a leader in an age of power and expansion, needs to consolidate his ranks. Should the new leaders forsake these qualities, turn stolid, rigid, and conformist, or indulge themselves in a struggle for power, then their downfall is certain. These are among the larger issues that will determine the future of the Communist leadership. Beyond this, any attempt to turn prophet is inadvisable.

Up to the time of their seizure of power in 1949, the Communists were carrying on a gigantic subversion. Since 1949 the Peking regime has been the established government of the country. With this change of front, there has been a marked increase in emphasis on the application of the Soviet system. Previously, as we have seen, during the period of subversion, the Communists threw into their melting-pot diverse influences culled from varying sources, from the Chinese Robin Hood tradition and practical field experiences as well as from certain useful elements of the Marxist doctrine. Now the problems confronting the Red leaders are different. The changed circumstances have led them to rely much more heavily on the introduction of the Soviet system of government organization and control. This trend may well become one of the decisive factors in the shaping of the new Chinese nation.

What this amounts to is a reversal of the historical process of Sinification. In past Chinese history, whenever a new power conquered an existing regime, it was, as a rule, a military victory, while politically and culturally the new power was assimilated by the old in a process of Sinification. In the present case, however, the supremacy of the old society has completely broken down. Not only has a superior military power destroyed the old regime, but the new power has brought with it an imported system of government and society to impose upon the old. Perhaps the only nearly comparable case was the Yuan (Mongol) conquest. After the Mongols subjugated China by their powerful hordes, they ruled China by an alien government which accepted little of China's traditions and institutions. The Mongols, however, had no superior means of control, but based their repressive rule on racial discrimination, which alienated the people and ultimately led to their downfall. In marked contrast, the Communists have put their emphasis on class discrimination. By championing the peasants and outlawing privilege, they have won the support of the masses. We are therefore witnessing a spectacle unparalleled in history. The imposition of a new type of control and the reversal of the process of Sinification go a long way to explain the distinctive political and sociological climate of China today.

In this reversal, of course, there are differences in the details of historical comparison. A further look into these differences may yield a greater insight into what is now happening in China. When the Hsiung-nu, Hsien-pi, T'o-ba, Tu-chüeh, Sha-to, Khitan, Tangut, and Juchen, the nomad tribes of the past, came into contact with China, Chinese culture had a corroding influence on the identity of the invaders, with the result that the Confucian ideology of the sedate agricultural society of China overcame the military prowess of the primitive nomads and led to their assimilation into the great melting-pot of China. The present Sovietization of China does not involve the undermining of military power by culture, but rather involves the defeat of one system of society by another. Thus it is not the military forces of China that have brought her to invade Russia and exposed her to Sovietization. Rather Communism has invaded China, through the medium of a new revolutionary movement within China herself, with the result that the same sedate agricultural society which acted so virulently as a conquering force in bygone ages now becomes the helpless target of attack by a doctrine of social upheaval specially suited to underdeveloped countries. But in this clash of different systems of society, China has not lost her identity, nor is the spirit of Chinese culture dead. Contrary to popular belief, Confucianism is by no means bankrupt. What has gone by default is the social

and economic props on which the Confucian society was
erected. There is no doubt that the traditional Chinese
society is undergoing a radical transformation following
the triumph of the Communists and the current spread of
Sovietization. But it is important to remember that this is
a revolution in the system of society, rather than the sub-
jugation of a nation by a superior culture. Unlike the
nomad tribes who were assimilated as a result of Sinification, China will remain China, but she will be a new and
different China.

Pre-eminent in the new type of control is the highly
organized machine of the Chinese Communist Party. It
is true that the handful of Red leaders, as discussed above,
are men of unusual perspicacity and determination. But
leading a revolution that has engulfed over five hundred
million people, it is doubtful whether they could have accomplished a great deal without the devotion and heroism
of the rank and file of the party. The party membership
was less than one million throughout the Kiangsi and
Yenan days. It was three million by 1949, the year the
Communists took over. By the close of 1954 it had reached
the six-million mark. The members of the Communist
Party are teams of picked men, phalanxes of trained
fighters, so to speak. The party cells and branches reach
the lowest levels of society. An iron discipline provides an
efficient chain of command. Devotion to the cause of the
party is almost a matter of life and death for the members.
To ensure maxium efficiency of operation, authority is
concentrated in the highest organs of the party, while
participation by the middle and lower strata is spread over
a wide area. Rather than accept a large number of members of questionable loyalty, the Communists have made

their party one of true revolutionary zeal. Under the Kuomintang, it is to be recalled, the same objective was sought; but party membership soon became a haven for non-revolutionary or anti-revolutionary politicians, and the spirit of revolution ceased to exist. The Communists have scrupulously avoided such an outcome. As I have said before, the Communists excelled in a qualitative rather than a quantitative sense. In the early days, Kuomintang persecution provided a sort of involuntary selective force for the Communist Party membership. Later, as members increased in number, the Cheng-feng movement in the early 1940's and the more recent "Three-anti Movement" (against corruption, waste, and bureaucratism) were launched to correct undesirable tendencies among the followers of the party. As a result, the party has remained pure and strong. During the enforcement of the Land Reform Law of 1950, the campaign against the "counter-revolutionaries" in 1951, and the vigorous "Five-anti Movement" to establish control over urban business classes in 1952, the work was performed entirely by the cadres of this powerful party. It is clear that this party, under the directives of Peking, is going to exercise over-all authority in governing the new China. In this connection, it is interesting to note that the Anglo-American educated students have not been given positions of power, though their technical abilities are being put to the use of the state under officers chosen from the party.

The development of the Chinese Communist Party into an organism for dynamic political action can best be appreciated by a comparison with China's previous experiences in secret societies and political parties. Throughout the centuries, the people of China formed secret societies for the redress of their grievances. Take, for instance, the Triad Society. While it had certain rudimentary methods of organization and a strong sense of fraternal bonds, its mystic ritual tended to cloud whatever program it had for social action. Moreover, its revolutionary activities, sporadic rather than systematic, remained in the underground stage. It also tended strongly to compromise and co-operate with the privileged groups of society; in fact, on numerous occasions it was utilized by the privileged groups to promote their interests.

Among the political parties, one may recall the Reform and Conservative parties of the Sung dynasty, the Tung Ling Party of the Ming dynasty, the Reform Party under the Ch'ing (Manchu) dynasty, and the various republican parties following the Revolution of 1911. These parties started out with well-defined platforms. But, as a rule, they suffered from a lack of substantial following among the people. In time they indulged in personal acrimonies rather than in battles over public issues. It was also characteristic of these parties that clannish relations and provincialism often crept in to create internal factions. The Kuomintang was many times better organized than these earlier parties. But even here membership was too heterogeneous to give it a true unity of mind and action. It, too, developed personal rivalries, which were further complicated by family relationships and regional alliances. It should be noted that whatever factional differences there were in the Communist Party occurred in the early years prior to unification of the leadership by Mao, while in the Kuomintang the unified leadership under Sun Yat-sen was short-lived and disintegrated into numerous factions and cliques in subsequent years.

In both its character and its operation, then, the Communist Party bears little resemblance to the political parties or secret societies of China's past history. Paradoxically enough, the feudal hierarchy of the Chou dynasty and the Confucian state cult in subsequent centuries are much more comparable. When the Chou arose in Shensi and carried out the political and military conquest of the rest of China, its machinery of control was the hierarchy of feudal nobles and sub-nobles who, relying upon the principles of feudal grant and hereditary succession, imposed effectively the control of the conquering minority upon the population of the country. Later, after Confucianism became the state cult, the scholar-literati replaced the feudal nobility and under the banners of Confucianism formed a new type of elite rule over the country. The Communist Party of today is not unlike those two systems in its essential spirit. It may safely be said that the factors responsible for the development of the Chinese Communist Party into a militant force included these: subordination to a monolithic system of control, maintenance of a rigorous discipline, purity of membership, and a goal-consciousness to impose the rule of the elite.

These are the qualities that have made the Communist Party a powerful force in the Chinese Revolution. But such qualities alone would not have sufficed if the human equation was not what it is in China. Absolute control is effectively wielded by the leadership of the elite because the people are not yet ready for self-government. This is an aspect of great importance in any consideration of the role played by the Chinese Communist Party. Communist methods would not have worked in the United States or Great Britain, but in China they operate with a telling

effect. The fact that the party is numerically small makes
no material difference. What counts is that it is the only
politically conscious group in a vast sea of humanity. This
explains why the Communist Party, by planting its cells
in every stratum of society and every walk of life, is able
to swing the entire country.

The rule of the Communist elite, moreover, is a straight
and unmixed proposition. It is not qualified in point
either of time or of space. Sun Yat-sen had also advocated
Kuomintang tutelage prior to ultimate democracy. But
such a conception of elite rule is conditional rather than
total. In point of space, where the Communist Party
strictly maintained its identity to the exclusion of the rest
of the society, the Kuomintang mingled with all social
groups, with the result that while one remained elite and
ruled, the other grew diffused and degenerated. In point
of time, the dictatorship of the Communist Party is un-
limited in duration, while the one-party rule of the Kuomintang was admittedly for a short term. The idea of
tutelage as a preparatory step to constitutional government
is a self-contradiction from the standpoint of elite rule and
manipulation of power. As things turned out, the Communists have succeeded where the Kuomintang has failed. In
the last analysis, then, the Communist elite rule is absolutist while the Kuomintang elite rule was moderate. But
the absolutist does not necessarily arouse opposition, just
as the moderate is not always popular. In an underdeveloped country like China, absolutism appears fit to conquer, while moderation simply leads to confusion and
decay.

Despite the constant use of the term "people's democracy," the system of government under Communist China

is anything but democratic. The trend is clearly one of tight centralization of control. With their characteristic facileness, the Communist leaders strive to conceal this totalitarianism by such phrases as "democratic centralism" and "democratic dictatorship." The definition of "democratic centralism" as given by Mao Tse-tung is as follows: "This system is at once democratic and centralized; that is to say, it is centralization on a democratic basis, and at the same time is democracy under centralized direction. This system alone can give expression to broad democracy by investing supreme power in the various grades of people's congresses; at the same time, it permits state affairs to be managed in a centralized manner, with the various grades of government doing the work entrusted to them by the various grades of people's congresses and safeguarding all the necessary democratic activities of the people." Chou En-lai's explanation of "democratic dictatorship" is that among the four classes that make up the people of China (that is, labor, peasantry, petty bourgeoisie, and national bourgeoisie), there is democracy, and that over the outlawed classes (that is, landlords, bureaucratic capitalists, and Kuomintang members), the people exercise dictatorship. Chou assures the world that the two are not contradictory but "work in unison."

A closer examination, however, reveals that what Chou means by democracy is in reality a sort of equalitarian status among the four classes that form the people of China, rather than popular sovereignty, much less the effective exercise of popular sovereignty. There is a general leveling of the people's rights and means of livelihood. But the power of government is strictly concentrated in the top leadership of the Communist Party. Mao lays great stress on investing supreme power in the people's congresses. But the crux of the matter is that the congresses are controlled by the party. Thus under the Communist government in China, democracy in the sense in which it is generally understood does not exist. "Centralism" or "dictatorship," however, is effective and real. The people are given an equalitarian status, but they do not have any control of the government, which is reserved exclusively for the Communist Party, particularly the Politburo of the party.

In Communist China today political freedom is denied the people. Such weapons of control as the police, surveillance by the party cadres, public accusation, and so on, are fully developed to stamp out any dissent or opposition. The Constitution of 1954, indeed, contains an elaborate bill of rights. But it has no meaning at all because the government reserves for itself the power to "suppress all counterrevolutionary and anti-state activities" and to "punish all traitors and counterrevolutionaries." The great spectacle of the elections of the people's congresses in the latter half of 1953 also made a mockery of the democratic process. Some 300,000 hsiang (administrative villages) held elections amid great publicity. But the hand of the party cadres was noted in every phase of the affair. Constituted as election committees under the government's orders, they supervised the registration of the electors, drew up the lists of nominees corresponding in number to those to be elected, and presided over the meetings for voting. The net result was complete stage-management by the party rather than free election. No one except the party nominee had a chance to win. In fact, the only function of an election was to rubber-stamp the orders handed down from above.

To the Western mind, it is unthinkable to found a new government on such a basis. The West, with its advanced experience in democracy, is fixed in its conception that any regime denying political rights and individual liberty to its people is a weak regime. It fails to see how such a regime as the Communist regime in China, suppressing popular aspirations and using ruthless methods, can flourish. The answer to this is of considerable interest. In the estimation of the Communists, the issue at stake in China today is the need for an effective central government that can maintain peace and unification and thereby give the people a decent livelihood. The Communists believe that a corrupt government, with or without democracy, will not be accepted by the people, but a clean and efficient government, even without democracy, can successfully be maintained. The strong points of the Communist position seem to be twofold: they have centralized political power not in a monarch or a personal dictator but in a state built on a revolutionary program that fits the economic and social conditions of the country, and they have taken military power away from local government and concentrated it in the hands of the central government. Under such a scheme, the anti-democratic rule is safely launched. Of course, they realize that good government plus democracy, if possible of achievement, would seriously endanger their hold. But since no force is yet in sight that is capable of offering such an ideal commonweal to the people of China, they are not afraid of the anti-democratic trend being effectively challenged.

The Western view of democracy may be valid from the standpoint of a long-range political process, but it is highly unreal, the Communists maintain, under the existing circumstances in China. Hence the Communists make it a point to prevent any corruption or abuses in government and to give the people an equalitarian status. The specific grievances and material needs of the people are taken care of. But beyond this every effort is made to consolidate the supremacy of Communist control. Absolute control from above is considered the only way to maintain the unified state, and unification is regarded as the greatest blessing to the people. The Communists seem to operate upon the premise that so long as they have helped the masses to satisfy their pressing needs, they are absolved of any obligation to observe the principle of popular sovereignty. As they lift the masses from utter poverty to a better living, from insecurity to peace, from virtual servitude to rejuvenation, the price they ask is a complete negation of democracy.

Here we see the re-enactment of the historical pattern of so many strong dynasties in China's great past. Once again a regime has risen to power because it has taken concrete measures to cope with the problem of the people's livelihood. But more than ever the rule is despotic and absolute. In this respect the Communist regime reaffirms the subtle continuity of certain concepts in Chinese governmental philosophy. For two thousand years the system of absolutist government prevailed in China with the aid of the Confucian philosophy of government, which stressed the point that people are naturally classified as the governing and the governed, that for the governed to obey the governing is the paramount virtue of man, and that as government is the business of the elite, the rights of the individual are of necessity subordinate to his social obligations. Since the founding of the Republic (1912), Western-educated leaders have endeavored to introduce democracy in opposition to this traditional philosophy. But the failures in this connection seem to have underscored by way of contrast the effectiveness of Confucian authoritarianism. Being shrewd readers of Chinese history, the Communists have resurrected the old system of absolutism in a new guise. Thus, in spite of the great social upheaval, and in spite of the unleashing of tremendous revolutionary energies, the Communist government today represents a retreat to the past. Like the absolutist government of the past, the Communist rule refuses to reckon with popular sovereignty. Along the entire path of their march to power, the Communists have expected the people to follow and to obey. Clearly, sometime and somewhere in the process of future evolution, this totalitarianism will clash with the genuine democratic aspirations of the people. But, for the moment, the Communist hypothesis seems to be entirely valid, and the colossus of Peking with its anti-democratic rule goes unchallenged.

The pattern of strong centralization of political control, however, is only one side of the picture. The regime in Peking is above all a great military power. In the foregoing chapters, we have discussed how, under Kuomintang persecution, the necessity of armed revolt was recognized by the Red leaders, and how their mastery of mass organizational methods helped the growth of the Red Army. It has been the basic belief of the Communists that unless they developed adequate armed strength in their own right, their very survival would be threatened. This is why in spite of the truce with the Kuomintang in 1937, the united front during the war with Japan, and all the formulas put forth during the mediation talks after V–J Day, the

Communists never yielded ground on the issue of their military strength. This complete reliance on military power is even stronger now in the minds of the leaders in Peking.

It is generally maintained that the major strength of the Communist army is their political indoctrination. There is no question that a greater degree of political consciousness exists among the rank and file of the Red Army than in the armies of the past. The basic difference, however, goes deeper than the mere imposition of party training or direction. Unlike the traditional armies of China, the Red Army is made of new material and dedicated to a new proposition. In the first place, it does not prey upon the public as did the mercenary troops of the past. To be a soldier in the Red Army is true military service, not a means of making a living for the unemployed, the social outcast, or the pauper. Second, the outlook of the Red soldier as well as of the officer is characterized by a sense of self-respect and public duty: they are to serve the state rather than to molest the people. Third, army commanders as power nuclei with ever-recurring tendencies of insubordination to the central government no longer exist. The troops are instruments of state policy, no longer the personal retainers of self-seeking generals. The sum total is that the Red Army is a genuine national army, representing the undissipated strength of the nation and subject to the supreme command of the central government. If there was ever a parallel in China's past history, the armies of the early Han and the early T'ang and the *Fu-pin* systems of the Northern Dynasties preceding the T'ang might be considered a close approximation. But even then a recognition of the dignity of the man in uniform and the loyalty of the armies to the state were not firmly established. Whatever faults may be observed in other directions, the emergence of the Red Army in its present capacity as a mighty instrument of national policy is an epoch-making event in Chinese history.

The military power of Communist China attained its vast dimensions after twenty years of development and growth. This was natural in view of the revolutionary tasks that were undertaken during the two decades. But with the seizure of power and unification of the country in 1949, a new era was inaugurated. The demands of a period of insurrection no longer existed. Accordingly, Peking had to decide whether it would reduce, maintain, or augment the strength of its armed forces. In past ages, whenever a new dynasty came to power, the wise ruler would embark on a program of arms reduction. Internally, he would seek peaceful rehabilitation—that is, an end to civil strife, lightening of the people's burdens, and increase in production. Externally, since China was surrounded by "have-not" nomad tribes, the ruler usually considered it cheaper to appease these tribes by subsidies and marriages than to launch punitive expeditions. Such expeditions would be undertaken only in times of extraordinary prosperity when vainglorious rulers, helped by the surplus wealth of the country, wished to show the prowess of the Empire. The norm of military policy was conservation and reduction of expenditure.

Communist China, however, has found this formula totally inapplicable. Instead of arms reduction, she has embarked on a program of arms expansion. At present she is maintaining a regular army of close to 5,000,000, plus a militia (home guard) of 14,000,000. This is not because

China is overflowing with wealth. In reality, she is tightening the belt of the people in order to sustain such extravagance. But the Communists consider that China's conditions today are greatly different from those of the past. As a safeguard against the possible rise of rebellions, they believe that a large and powerful army is absolutely essential. They are aware that the emotions engendered by this great social upheaval are fraught with dangerous possibilities. Should any mistake lead to a reaction, its power for revenge would be tremendous. The only way to guard against such a retribution, remote though it may be, is the maintenance of a decidedly superior military power. Similarly, to maintain her new world position in the midst of stronger and potentially unfriendly rivals, Communist China feels the compelling need to keep her military strength at an astronomical height. In any event, with their totalitarian system of government, the Red leaders would not feel secure without huge armies as props for their power. Thus, instead of conservation or reduction, Communist policy since 1949 has put an increased emphasis on military power.

The manner in which Communist China increased her armed strength has been, to say the least, unusual. Ever since its inception, the Red Army has followed an unconventional course in its growth. It faced no difficulty in obtaining manpower, but was consistently handicapped by the lack of equipment. The contemptuous epithet *"wu ho chih chung"* ("haphazard conglomeration of black crows") used by the Kuomintang to designate Communist troops, while understimating their morale, certainly reflected correctly the strange miscellany of equipment carried by the initial mobile bands. This serious weakness was remedied by extraordinary means. In the very early days of peasant uprisings, the Communist bands seized the arms of the village peace-preservation corps to equip themselves. During Kiangsi days, they captured large quantities of arms and ammunition from the Kuomintang forces, just as in the subsequent decade of war with Japan they increased their strength by preying on the Japanese forces. The story of tremendous quantities of modern American arms of the Kuomintang divisions falling into the hands of the Red Army during the great civil war of 1947–9 is familiar to all. This growth in strength by utilizing stores of arms captured from opponents on the battlefield forms a curious epic in contemporary Chinese military history.

After the achievement of internal unification, Communist China was more determined than ever to increase the strength of the Red Army. For while it defeated the Kuomintang forces, certainly the Red Army in 1949–50 could hardly have been considered the army of a first-rate modern power. How to increase its size, augment its equipment, and improve its fighting power thus became the paramount task of the Red leaders upon the achievement of victory. Chinese history is full of instances wherein the maintenance of a large army was not compatible with the interests of peaceful reconstruction. To maintain a large army with a high fighting power often resulted either in depleting the treasury (such as was the experience of the Sung dynasty, the early Republic, and the Kuomintang period) or in imposing such crushing burdens on the people that they provoked widespread revolt (such as was the experience of the Ch'in and the Sui dynasties).

The problems faced by the Communists in 1949–50 were not unlike those faced by the rulers of these earlier periods. What has enabled the Red leaders to solve the problem with such apparent ease and success? Mao and his colleagues appear to be guided by the old adage that an army must be kept busy to be strong. The Red leaders after 1949 desired neither to demobilize nor to see the army rot in idleness. Instead, they looked for opportunities where they could be "gainfully employed."

The calculations underlying the Chinese intervention in Korea in 1950 were numerous and complicated. The conclusion of the Sino-Soviet Alliance and the resultant strategy of Peking and Moscow will be considered in a subsequent chapter. But viewed from the standpoint of the Communists' desire to improve and expand their military power, what happened behind the scenes throughout the Korean episode raises points of unusual interest. While it is not known whether the Peking regime committed itself to a plan of active intervention during the talks between Mao and Stalin in 1949–50, it is clear that Peking gave prompt and active support to the invasion move by the North Koreans, that the sudden appearance of Chinese "volunteers" *en masse* could not have taken place without adequate preparedness, and that the truce talks were dragged out over a long time by the tardiness of Peking to end the conflict. In the Korean war, Peking found a good chance to keep the Red Army busy and strong. The effectiveness of this calculation was borne out by bursts of popular enthusiasm inside China and the consequent swelling of the ranks of the Red Army. As a result of the Korean intervention, the over-all power of Red China's army not only was unaffected by the casualties, but actually increased in strength. The regular army grew from 2,500,000 men at the beginning of the Korean war to 5,000,000 at its close.

New officers were developed, and better fighting quality was achieved by an intensified training program. Above all, the size of the "People's Militia" rose to the high point of 14,000,000.

Meanwhile, Russian arms and advice helped considerably in carrying out a fast modernization of equipment. The ground force acquired firepower on the Western scale through its organized artillery, while a sizable air force was also created. By the close of the Korean war, China's land forces were fully comparable to those of a major Western power. Thus the Communists, again by adopting a purely expedient course designed to achieve what was best for their rule, succeeded in pushing the Red Army one step farther in its expansion. This strategy of augmenting Communist military power by keeping the army busy and by stimulating popular enthusiasm for the "glorious deeds of the People's Army" has its significance in any appraisal of Red China's motivations.

In the opinion of experts, the evolution of the Chinese Communist army has passed its most trying stage, and its future outlook is bright. From an army with substandard equipment, it has now become one with up-to-date firepower. True, many new problems will continue to challenge the Red leaders, not the least of which is the problem of keeping up with the international race in nuclear weapons. None the less, building on the base it has now, the Red Army will keep itself strong with relative ease. Under the latest conscription law, a dual process of demobilization and recruitment is in effect, whereby veterans are retired to join worker forces or resettled in rural areas while young recruits are brought in to fill the ranks of the army. The numbers involved in each of the periodic turnovers are very large. One obvious result is the extensive spread of military training among the people. Another— and more significant—result is the changing composition of the Red Army. Hitherto the Red Army has taken its men from the poor peasants. Now the fresh recruits come from all sectors of the population. Since few families are rich, young people conscripted from non-agricultural families begin to share the same outlook as that held by the revolutionary veterans of yesterday. Thus the sociological background of the Red Army is changing; its effect is to broaden the peasant base into a nationwide base. In this process of bringing in youth from non-agricultural families, the Red Army converts them at the same time that it trains them to be useful soldiers of the Communist state. After not too many years the control of the Red Army over the entire population of China will be complete. The leavening process going on in the Chinese army today is not unlike that which occurred in the Revolutionary Army of the American colonies. What began as an insurrectionary force grew with the spread of the Revolution into an army of all classes. In the homogenizing process of integrating the new army with a new society, the youth of Communist China, like those of the Thirteen Colonies, are fired by a spirit of self-reliance, a buoyancy born of a new social environment, and confidence in their new strength and destiny. An invading army sent against such a military power would be hard-pressed to escape defeat.

While rigid political control and increase in military strength are the twin tentacles of the power of the new regime in Peking, they deal only with the tangible matters of the present. What about the intangible and the future? Popular discontent need not raise its head in the form of rebellion: it can make its influence felt through the spread of ideas. The masses today may submit willingly to the strong government of Peking. But as years go by, there is no guarantee that corroding forces will not creep in to undermine the present edifice of power. The Communists do not have to look far afield to detect such possible dangers. Throughout Chinese history, the appeal of the Confucian scholars to the golden rule of the past has been used as a potent weapon to attack an existing regime. Furthermore, the influx of Western democratic thinking has also provided the Chinese people with ample ammunition for attacking a totalitarian regime like the Communist government.

To forestall the spread of dissident ideas, the Communists accordingly have made it their policy to destroy all traditional culture and institutions as well as Western educational influences. The crusade to wipe out the old heritage of the people is incredibly violent. In every sense, the Communists of today deserve the scathing epithet *"min chiao tsui jen"* ("criminals committing sacrilege against the teachings of the sages"). While there is no burning of books, all publications are government-controlled. "Reactionary" materials in school curricula are replaced by the Communist Party catechism. A mass sales campaign to acquaint the people with the teachings of Mao and Marx, Lenin and Stalin, is being hammered into the minds of every man and woman, while the more educated strata, having stronger associations with the old culture, are subjected to an intensive program of "brainwashing." This feverish activity on the part of the Communists is no doubt based upon the belief that the incessant pounding of a new ideology into the minds of the people will eventually uproot the old culture. Of course, the end result of this unrelenting process of thought-control is fear, uniformity, and general apathy. But the party leaders and cadres are being guided by an overriding desire to tear down the old—so much so that they consider their purpose well served so long as dissidence and heresy do not arise.

Part and parcel of this crusade against traditional values is the campaign to break down family loyalties. It is general knowledge that until the Communist seizure of power, the clan or family was the most powerful institution in Chinese society. When it originated in antiquity, the clan was logically important because it was the indispensable basis for the feudal system of government during the Chou dynasty. Even after the demise of the feudal system, however (several hundred years before the Christian era), the clan remained a powerful institution among the Chinese people. This was due to the lack of interest on the part of the monarchy in organizing the masses or building a national state. Accordingly, the Chinese people were more aware of their obligations to the head of the clan or family than to the state.

The Communists are now determined to put an end to this regard for the clan. In the new order, where the government effectively controls the people, there is no room left for the family or clan. Loyalty is to be singular, not plural. Where the family used to claim the allegiance of the individual, today the party (and through it the government) has stepped in to command that allegiance. Thanks to the impact of a decade of war, which dislocated the economic and social bases of the family and imposed broader problems than the family could solve, the Communists are meeting with great success in destroying the time-honored solidarity of the clan. Throughout the villages and cities, youngsters not only are breaking away from their family ties but are openly repudiating their parents and relatives. Time is running out for millions of elders looking vainly for a token payment of filial piety. China, which has revered age, has suddenly turned inhospitable to it. Behind this heartbreaking spectacle, the pillars of the old order are being swept away by the onrushing tide of iconoclasm and social change.

This destructive aspect of the gigantic effort of the Communists to preserve their power is matched by a somewhat more constructive aspect. As they look into the future, the Communist leaders are not oblivious of the greatest challenge yet to come: the question of the perpetuation of loyalty to the regime. To cope with this situation, Peking has been focusing its major attention on the training of youth. Feverish programs of education and indoctrination are now going on in Communist China, the aim of which is to turn all the young people into ardent followers of Communism. The Communists openly state that they have no use for people over thirty. Instead, they concentrate their efforts on those below that age, who, they believe, can still be shaped to the Communist mold and thus turned into faithful supporters of the new regime. In the Ideological Remolding Campaign of 1951–2, agitations were deliberately fomented on college campuses and among professional groups. In these high-strung agitations, students were incited to rise against their teachers, younger members of the staff to rise against the older ones. Peking's overall purpose is to recast the educational system, giving the lead to the young people who are more prone to carry out the wishes of the Communist Party. Not only are the young people taught the Communist creed, but they are made to understand that all branches of learning must have a useful function for the state. They are taught that the individual exists for the sake of the state, that learning is not for learning's sake but has to be utilitarian and patriotic. After such training, the new partisans are given positions of responsibility, and, subject to party orientation, are given full scope to develop their creative talents and impulses.

How far can the Red leaders win over the younger generation and how completely can they shut the Chinese youth away from influences beyond the "bamboo curtain" —these are the questions that will determine whether Communism's hold on posterity is to be a success or a failure. For this reason, it would be the height of folly to deride Peking's emphasis on youth. It has been estimated that well over sixty per cent of the veteran leaders of the Chinese Communist movement were students to begin with. These youthful adherents have been of great value to the Revolution because they are forward-looking; their enthusiasms have not been worn thin by hard experience; and they appear capable of winning popular confidence. To encourage them to give expression to their energies and utilize those energies is proving a useful policy. In striking contrast, the Kuomintang through its twenty years in power provided little outlet for the emotions and talents of young people. It was burdened with the "old guard," whose members did not choose to relinquish their influence or share it with younger men. The Communists have no intention of withering on the vine: growing old and losing popular appeal are synonyms in their political dictionary. Hence they encourage, nurture, and exalt youth. There is no denying the fact that here again the Communists are tapping a tremendous source of new strength. The leaders of Peking well understand that two or three decades from now, when the boys and girls of today come of age, they will hold the center of the stage and must therefore be well equipped to carry on the unfinished tasks.

IV

THE DRIVE FOR GREAT–POWER STATUS

❀

In the preceding chapters our discussion of the emergence of a new age in China has been confined to the domestic aspects of the revolution led by the Communists. But of equally great concern both to the Chinese people and to the peoples of the world has been the international impact of the rise of the Communist regime. China has suddenly transformed herself from a weak sub-colonial country into a strong modern world power. Within a surprisingly short period of time she has made her influence felt in almost every corner of the globe. This phenomenal revolution in China's external relations may well be the capital fact in the metamorphosis of world politics of the mid-twentieth century. Accordingly, this chapter will examine the character and extent as well as the meaning of this revolution.

The fundamental force motivating Communist China's new role in international affairs is her militant nationalism. Once again it is essential to recall that for the first time since the decline of the Manchu dynasty the Communists have achieved unification in China. As a result of this unification, China has become the strongest and the most assertive power in Asia. From the breeding-ground of international rivalries and exploitation, she has transformed herself into a center of potent leadership. This is the central fact one must bear in mind in approaching the problem of China. It is the expansive energy of the new regime seeking to assert its new power and position and its uncompromising challenge in advancing a new balance of power in the Far East that have produced the holocaust in world affairs that we are witnessing.

Because of the far-reaching implications inherent in such a situation, the revolution in China's external relations has created a wide range of problems, despite the short period of its existence. Things have happened fast on China's international front since 1949. The central thread of development, however, has been the powerful drive to win big-power status. For the sake of a clear perspective, it is advisable to deal with the evolution of Communist China's foreign relations from this standpoint. A great complex of psychological and emotional reactions, driven by a new nationalism, has spearheaded this great upheaval in her international relations. Among these reactions, one notes especially a strong sense of emancipation from oppression and an eagerness to overcome past humiliations, a great outburst of national pride, tinged with frequent shows of arrogance, a tendency to saber-rattling and demagoguery, and a plain xenophobia. Behind the façade of this provocative mood, however, deeper and more permanent currents have caused the leaders in Peking to run the entire gamut of old and new devices in international diplomacy with the constant objective of fighting for a positive acknowledgment of China as one of the great world powers. During the early stages of this chain of dramatic moves, which were marked by aggressive expansion, hostility to the United States, and calculated ef-

forts to heighten tension, China tried vainly to accomplish
her purpose by forcing the submission of the United States
and the Western nations to her demands. In the more recent phase of her policy, however, she appears to have
changed her approach. The new policy has been to achieve
big-power status by first initiating direct talks with the
United States and then obtaining the satisfaction of her
demands by peaceful means.

To begin with, Communist China's militant nationalism
has its origins in the eight years of war against Japan. Prior
to that war, Chinese nationalism had a history of about
thirty years. But those were years of weakness for China,
and the budding spirit of nationalism failed to thrive. As
we have already seen, the doctrine of nationalism preached
by Sun Yat-sen sought to free China from the imperialist
yoke by the abolition of the unequal treaties and the attainment of a position of equality in the family of nations.
But it was a hapless struggle. With no unification, no
peace, and no prosperity to back up her crusade against
imperialism, the powers listened to China's aspirations but
made no move to satisfy them. At the Versailles and Washington conferences, China was bitterly disappointed by the
standpat policies of the powers. Later, following the success of the Northern Expedition of the Kuomintang, there
was a brief period when the powers were more disposed to
turn a sympathetic ear to China's demands. This again,
however, vanished into thin air with the deepening of the
civil war between the Kuomintang and the Communists.
By the time Japan struck to conquer China, Chinese nationalism had achieved little of substantial value. But the
eight years of war (1937–45) altered the situation completely. It was in this life-and-death struggle and in the ul-

timate victory over the imperialist enemy that Chinese nationalism at last became a great driving force. Just as Japan's invasion was the climax of a century of imperialist oppression, so was her defeat a symbol of the end of an era of humiliation. The outcome of the war gave China independence, freedom, and strength.

In view of these circumstances, it is small wonder that Communist China has found the courage and the persistence to seek a new deal in her international relations. Not only has Peking experienced a strong sense of deliverance from the oppression of the imperialist powers, but the gloom and infamy of being prey to those powers have been replaced by an exhilarating feeling of dignity. In place of the ineptitude of the last thirty years, Chinese nationalism has forged a determination to restore greatness to the new nation and to make it the leading power in Asia. The leaders in Peking, after winning the war against Japan, a nation never before defeated in modern times, seem to have operated on the premise that they could do anything with Chinese nationalism if they worked hard at it. This is why Peking has been sensitive to any move that appeared inimical to her aspirations. She has had little inclination to make concessions. She has been exerting an increasing pressure for concrete acknowledgment of her strength and supremacy in Asia.

This fighting mood arising from Peking's new nationalism immediately raises the question: where does it find its targets of attack and what are they? As far as the realities of a century of imperialist exploitation are concerned, it must be emphasized that they were virtually wiped out by the end of World War II. To be sure, the departure of Germany from the Chinese scene after World War I and the renunciation of czarist Russia's rights and interests by the Soviet government still left the majority of the imperialist powers entrenched in China with their unequal treaties. But beginning with 1928, they abandoned certain special rights, as was evidenced in the regaining of tariff autonomy by China. Then came the sweeping changes made during World War II. The remaining features of the unequal treaties—particularly extraterritoriality and foreign settlements—were liquidated before the war ended. Not only had the Japanese attack completely undermined the positions of the imperialist powers, but as allies with China in a global war against the Axis powers, the nations concerned generally acknowledged that the old treaty rights should no longer be allowed to infringe upon the independence and sovereignty of China. By the time the Communists came to power, the old edifice of imperialist oppression in China had been practically destroyed. The Communists had little difficulty in liquidating whatever remained in the form of foreign business interests and holdings and foreign missionary establishments. Thus, as far as the removal of past grievances was concerned, it must be said that there existed no valid target of attack by the new nationalism. If China's aspirations, as originally envisaged under the influence of Sun Yat-sen, were to throw off the unequal treaties imposed in the last century by the imperialist powers, then the situation that the Communists found following their accession to power could hardly have constituted a cause for further conflict.

This, however, is not at all the way Peking views the situation. It is for this reason that the psychological reactions inhering in her militant nationalism are of absorbing interest and significance. Even though the concrete grievances against the imperialist powers have been removed, the very fact of their existence in history appears to justify the Communist leaders in making them targets of renewed attack. Accordingly, Peking's diplomacy has been marked by an eagerness to avenge past humiliations, to "turn the table," so to speak, against the powers. On the eve of the establishment of the Peking regime, Mao Tsetung made an illuminating statement. Quoting Chu Hsi, the Sung philosopher, who once remarked: "Apply to anyone the method he has first used on others," Mao told the Chinese people: "This is what we are doing. That is, to apply to imperialism and its lackeys . . . the same method with which they treated others. Simply this and nothing else!" The objective of the Peking regime, then, has been to "punish the imperialists" rather than merely to redress past grievances. This basic line of thinking goes a long way to explain the conduct of Peking's foreign policies. Chou En-lai's vitriolic blasts and his roughshod strategy, his skillful blending of threat, suspense, and cool calculation, demonstrated repeatedly in diplomatic duels with the West, are typical examples of the fact that the fortunes of the nations have come full circle in China.

In the wake of their successful seizure of power, the Communists have also displayed an unrestrained national pride and arrogance. This has been notable in all the major diplomatic events involving China since 1949. In the violent anti-American campaign, facts and merits have been ignored in order to give free play to the national ego. The reason that the United States has been the butt of such bitter hatred is not that she is the real culprit, but rather that attacking a great nation like the United States seems the best way to meet China's own pretensions. When Great

Britain extended diplomatic recognition to Peking, the latter treated it with a studied indifference, the inference being that she cared little for the favor of a great Western power. Peking's approach to the United Nations is equally interesting. While she minced no words in attacking the United Nations when branded the aggressor in the Korean war, she quickly upheld the visit of the Secretary-General to Peking in connection with the case of the American airmen as proof of China's growing international prestige. Peking also has made capital of the fact that on every important state occasion an impressive assemblage of leaders from foreign countries pays tribute to the new government. Never before in China's past periods of imperial greatness has the sense of national pride and prestige been raised to so high a point.

Underlying all these manifestations, there has been the constant threat of a resort to force against the Western powers. The nationalist program of Sun Yat-sen meant a crusade to emancipate China from foreign oppression, but its real object was to secure for China a position of equality in the family of nations. The emphasis was on peaceful co-operation. Now the new nationalism appears to be radically different in spirit. Having achieved emancipation and equality, it has adopted the technique of holding up the specter of war to the powers of the West. In other words, Communist China has been in a challenging rather than a tractable mood. The component elements of this belligerent mood include a variety of impulses and attitudes. First, there is no denying the fact that the Communists are intoxicated with success. Victory over Japan and over the Kuomintang has planted in their minds a mystic faith in their own invincibility. Second, the Communist line has inculcated in them the idea that they must not content themselves with the overthrow of imperialism in China, but should aim, as their ultimate objective, at waging a war against "world imperialism" until the latter is completely blotted out. These sentiments, stressed by Mao Tse-tung himself, have given an added fillip to an already blustering chauvinism. Third, it should be borne in mind that since the Chinese Communist movement has been nurtured by leaders who understand little or nothing of the spirit of Anglo-American civilization, the new nationalism is tinged with a strong anti-West bias. The high-handed actions taken against American nationals, including government representatives, have almost assumed the proportions of an anti-foreign mania.

The psychology of Peking's new nationalism has been dealt with at some length because more than anything else it enables us to understand the peculiar climate under which China has been conducting herself in her relations with the rest of the world. Of course, Peking's arrogance has its parallel in China's past epochs of greatness, especially in the Han and T'ang dynasties. But while the Han and the T'ang, in the international conditions of their time, could afford to show arrogance toward their nomad neighbors, Peking must realize that present-day China needs to live among the civilized nations of the world with some degree of reason, decency, and law. The fact that she has persisted in a course which offers continuous irritants creating tension with the West, points to the logical deduction that the acts of the new nationalism have been studied moves intended to accomplish not only a complete break with the past years of weakness but a revolutionary upturn in China's external affairs. With this picture in mind, we can proceed to discuss the concrete measures by which Peking has sought to implement her foreign policy.

The development of Peking's foreign policy since the establishment of the regime in 1949 may be considered in four major phases: (1) conclusion of the Sino-Soviet Alliance in February 1950 and the establishment of the basic policy of alignment with Russia and hostility toward the United States; (2) aggressive expansion into certain specific areas beyond China's periphery in an effort to extend China's control and influence; (3) an ambitious plan to acquire hegemony over Asian nations, coupled with a war of nerves waged as a means of gaining great-power status through international pressure on the United States; and (4) an awakening to the dangers in the overplay of tension, and initiation of a different strategy to win new international status through negotiation with the United States.

The conclusion of the Sino-Soviet Alliance following the extended visit of Mao Tse-tung to Moscow in the winter of 1949–50 must be regarded as the greatest event in modern Chinese diplomatic history. The Treaty of Shimonoseki (1895) and the Boxer Protocol (1901), of course, marked the nadir of China's humiliation, threatening as they did the breakup of the Chinese Empire at the turn of the century. The Washington Conference of 1921–2 and the Sun-Joffe Manifesto of 1924 were indeed halfway points in the rejuvenation of the Chinese people. But the great upsurge of nationalism had to await China's attainment of big-power strength to give it full expression. The Sino-Soviet Alliance overshadows by far any of the events just noted. Marking the high point of half a century of ferment, the consummation of this alliance symbolized the coming of

an era in Chinese diplomacy when she could deal with the
world powers as their equal.

The guiding spirit of this alliance is a firm bond between China and Soviet Russia and a hostility toward the
United States and the other Western nations. In the three
basic documents signed on February 14, 1950 (Treaty of
Friendship, Alliance, and Mutual Assistance; Agreement
on the Chinese Changchun Railway, Port Arthur, and
Dairen; and Agreement on Credits to China) this spirit
underlies most of the provisions. The treaty, effective for
thirty years, pledges the two contracting parties to the use
of all necessary measures for "preventing a repetition of
aggression and violation of the peace on the part of Japan
or any other State uniting with Japan, directly or indirectly, in acts of aggression." Should either party be attacked by Japan or any state allied with Japan, the other
party will immediately render military and other assistance. Both parties pledge themselves not to conclude any
alliance against the other, and to "consult each other in
regard to all important international problems affecting
the common interests of the Soviet Union and China."
The second document provides for the transfer by Soviet
Russia to Chinese ownership of all its rights to joint administration of the Chinese Changchun Railway, and for
the withdrawal of Soviet troops from Port Arthur, following the signing of a peace treaty with Japan or in any
event not later than the end of 1952. The agreement on
credits extends to China a credit of $300,000,000 at low
interest over a five-year period to help restore China's
economy. Upon the signing of the documents, Chou En-
lai declared that "the friendship, alliance, and mutual assistance between China and the Soviet Union are sealed

now with the signed treaty. The imperialist bloc headed
by American imperialism resorted to all kinds of provocative methods attempting to frustrate the friendship between our Powers, but these ignominious attempts have
failed utterly."

The momentous nature of this event struck the West
with a tremendous impact. Yet the Chinese Communist
leaders had warned all along of their determination to take
this drastic step. As early as 1940, Mao Tse-tung had put
forth his theory that the world is divided between the socialist and imperialist camps, and that since China has been
oppressed by the imperialist camp, she must join the socialist camp. On July 1, 1949, three months prior to the
establishment of the Peking government, Mao openly
urged the "lean to one side" policy. He said: "The forty
years' experience of Sun Yat-sen and the twenty-eight years'
experience of the Communist Party have made us firmly
believe that, in order to win victory and to consolidate victory, we must lean to one side. . . . One either leans to
the side of imperialism or to the side of socialism. Neutral-
ity is camouflage, and a third road does not exist." Such
words of warning were not heeded by the West. It was the
hope of the West at the time that the Communists when
coming to power might turn to co-operation with the
West.

As things turned out, however, it is doubtful whether
Mao and his associates gave such co-operation serious consideration. At that time the Communist-Kuomintang struggle had reached its greatest intensity. It was natural that
the United States should work with and help the established government of China in the early postwar years.
But since Mao's avowed policy was the elimination of

General Chiang Kai-shek and the utter destruction of Kuomintang power, his turning away from the United States should not have been entirely unexpected. The speeches made by Mao in this connection left little doubt of his views: "We are also grateful to Britain and the United States, particularly the latter, for their immense contribution to the common cause—the defeat of the Japanese aggressor. . . . But we ask the United Nations governments, particularly the British and the United States governments, to pay serious attention to the voice of the overwhelming majority of the Chinese people . . . so as to avoid impairing our friendship or losing the friendship of the Chinese people. Any foreign government that helps the Chinese reactionaries to stop the Chinese people's pursuit of democracy will be committing a grave error."

In the last stages of the war against the Kuomintang, the Communists stepped up their anti-American campaign. After the establishment of the new government in Peking, Mao left forthwith for Moscow. There was not even the faintest sign of an attempt to explore the possibilities of normal diplomatic relations with the United States. Later, when Great Britain extended recognition, Peking treated it with a casualness tantamount to a studied affront, as noted above. It cannot be plainer, then, that Peking had decidedly made up her mind to ally herself with Soviet Russia.

It is important to recognize the reasons that led the Communist leaders to a firm policy decision like this. Could it have been as simple and as abstract as Mao put it? Presumably, the Communists had determined upon an alliance with Russia because to them there existed no third road besides socialism and imperialism. Leaning toward

Russia was therefore imperative unless China were to choose the imperialist camp. While this line makes good theorizing, it is extremely unlikely that Communist policy was actually decided upon a basis of such outright abstractions. Inasmuch as the Communists are great realists, their decision to ally themselves with Soviet Russia must be accounted for on a different basis.

Probably one of the most telling factors is the simple matter of geography. Russia and China are neighbors. For thousands of miles, their frontiers touch. Russia is in every respect closer to China than is the United States or any other Western power. Until China's strength has grown so that she can stand alone, this long and exposed land frontier in the north, northwest, and northeast will no doubt give Russia a leverage in her dealings with China that far surpasses that of their common ideology. With the state of their strength as it was in 1949–50, it took no special acumen for the Red leaders in Peking to realize that if they broke with Russia or "leaned away" from her, the latter could if she chose move in over their common borders or, at the very least, maintain a tight hold on the border provinces of Manchuria and Sinkiang. She could also put obstacles in the way of the new government in Peking, thereby threatening the very momentum of the Revolution. In the event of such a disastrous state of affairs, the West would no doubt give moral support to China's cause, but it would hardly come to her rescue by military means. Such a prospect must have appeared particularly frightening to the newly established government in Peking. It is not too much to say that the aspirations of the Communists could have been brought to naught by such a turn of events. On the other hand, were Red China to direct her hostility to the West, it was fairly safe to assume that the West would not attack her. The Western powers were interested in trade with China. Geographical distances were such as to make the idea of an invading armada from across the seas utterly incredible. The flippant epithet "paper tiger," which the Communists used to designate the United States in their recurring tirades, was the best reflection of their belief that the United States would not go to war with China except under the gravest of provocations.

It is true that the United States has figured large in Chinese affairs in the past half-century. But it is Soviet Russia, rather than the United States, that can in times of crisis do mortal harm to China. The Communist leaders did not have to look far afield to find a reminder of this stark reality. Soviet occupation of Manchuria at the end of the war with Japan wrought great havoc to the industrial establishments there. A great portion of the capital stock was dismantled and carried off. As is well known, China's heavy industries were concentrated chiefly in that one area. To antagonize Russia, so the Communists reasoned, would have meant the loss of an overwhelming portion of the nation's industrial potential. On the other hand, a policy of friendship could result in the restoration of an industrial sector comparable to that of postwar India or that of Japan in the early 1920's. Accordingly, the realities in the situation led China to conclude that it was to her interest to align herself with Russia.

As for Russia, the rise of the Chinese Communists to power has offered her the perfect opening to fulfill her agelong ambition in the Far East—an unchallenged influence over China. Molotov said in 1950 that next to Rus-

sia's October Revolution the triumph of the Chinese Communists was the biggest blow to "the whole system of world
imperialism and all present-day plans for imperialist aggression." While this was no doubt true from the standpoint of the strategy of world Communism, it hardly revealed the true face of Russia where China alone was
concerned. Molotov's elation was prompted by the prospect
that China would now move within the orbit of Soviet
designs. Here, too, the issue involved was a matter of the
sordid realities of power politics rather than of the abstractions of Communist ideology.

Through the centuries, the paramount aim of Russia,
whether under the czarist government or under the Soviet
regime, has not been territorial occupation *per se* but
rather the pursuit of a degree of control which would prevent China from aligning herself with foreign powers coming to her from beyond her eastern shores. During the
past hundred years, however, Russia's designs were continuously frustrated. Being outmaneuvered, she had no recourse but to grab whatever she could to counterbalance
the gains of the rival powers. The events of 1858, 1881, and
1898, when Russia obtained substantial gains in the Amur
region, Turkistan, and the Liaotung Peninsula, were mile-
stones in this line of action. The entente of 1924 seemed to
hold out greater promise for the fulfillment of her ambition, but after a brief period this hope waned with the ex-
pulsion of the Communists by the Kuomintang. Thus Russian ambitions in China never found fulfillment. Her
plans formed a bizarre pattern of advances and retreats—
all aimed at achieving an exclusive influence over political
and economic affairs in China. Russia would send troops to
occupy border regions and put pressure on the Chinese au-

thorities when they yielded too many concessions to the Western powers; but then she would evacuate her forces as soon as the rival powers relaxed their own pressures on China. None of these moves, however, brought the desired result.

The consummation of the Sino-Soviet Alliance must be viewed, then, as opening the way for the ultimate triumph of this agelong ambition on the part of Russia. Up to 1949, the succession of Chinese governments—Manchu, early Republican, and finally Kuomintang—maintained close relations with all the foreign powers. Now, for the first time, the Communist regime, prompted by the considerations outlined above, was disposed to follow the "lean to one side" policy. This is what caused Molotov to declare boastfully that the treaty of February 1950 "transformed Sino-Soviet friendship into a great and mighty force for consolidating universal peace such as has no equal and has never had an equal in human history." What Molotov really meant was that Russia could foresee that as a result of this alliance with China, those rival powers which Russia had always regarded as obstacles to the promotion of her interests would be barred from China.

So long as this alignment achieves a new balance of power in the Far East, Russian interests will be eminently served and she may be expected to implement her obligations under the alliance scrupulously. This is the underlying reason why Russia was satisfied to restore Manchuria to the Communists, why she extended military and economic aid to them, and why she withdrew her troops from Port Arthur. Of course, the leverage that the present economic and military aid gives to Russia falls far short of the degree of influence which she coveted in pre-Communist days, but it does serve to bind China closely to the Soviet bloc. This brings to one's mind the famous—or infamous— Amau declaration of 1934, warning the Western powers to keep their hands off China. Japan may have been the author of this declaration, but Russia is its true practitioner today. When Japan spoke on that score, she brought upon herself the opprobrium of the entire world. But Russia is quietly reaping the harvest, with the world hardly realizing that she is implementing those very notorious principles propounded by the Gaimusho.

There are other aspects of the Alliance which deserve our attention. It is important to remember that while China was motivated by geopolitical reasons in coming closer to Russia, and Russia was animated by the ambition to draw China into the Russian orbit, China did not approach the Kremlin in the role of a vassal nor did Russia treat her as such. After all, the Chinese Communists have built up their strength in their own right. In fact, down to the eve of the great civil war of 1947–9, Russian policy toward the Chinese Communists was one of passive blessing rather than active aid. Certainly Mao did not depend on Soviet military power to "put him on the throne," as Shih Chin-t'ang relied on the Khitans during the Five Dynasties (early tenth century) or Wang Ching-wei on the Japanese during World War II. Mao's rise to power has been characterized by a great independence of spirit and struggle. Thus it would be an error to regard Mao as a puppet. Yet, there is no denying the fact that the thirty-year treaty fills a crying need of the new regime in Peking. Clearly Mao would not be the formidable figure he is today if he did not have the backing of this epoch-making alliance.

Another important aspect of the matter is that the Alliance is frankly conceived as a grand coalition of the vast resources of the two nations for both defensive and offensive purposes. Geographically, this colossus not only spans the greater part of Asia and Europe, but operates from the central axis of the Eurasian heartland, which in the nature of geostrategy lends a peculiar strength to both partners. In terms of manpower and productive capacity, this great coalition is even more significant. Not only can the combination of Soviet military matériel and Chinese manpower create a giant army in time of war, but in a peacetime build-up the abundance of cheap labor in China can serve to accelerate production, thereby adding considerably to whatever assistance is received from Russia. The alliance is thus a stupendous undertaking on a stupendous scale. Each side has great internal strength, plus a will to utilize it for the coalition. Each has substantial assets to put into the pool. Most significant of all, the contributions of both sides complement one another. One may therefore conclude that this alliance between Soviet Russia and Communist China is not at all comparable to the relations between Russia and her satellite countries. In the case of the satellites of eastern Europe, for instance, their ties to Soviet Russia are ties between the Lilliputian and the Gargantuan, and for that reason those ties do not possess the might of the Sino-Soviet Alliance. In this case, both signatories are strong, and each desires to consummate the treaty out of a recognition of the power of the other contracting party. Because the alliance rests on a basis of equality rather than on a suzerain-vassal relationship, it has developed into the most potent force in the world affairs of our time.

Since the contracting parties approach each other on a

basis of equality, the resultant accord is, of necessity, a partnership of mutual advantage. Let us recapitulate the benefits to each of the signatories. The importance of the alliance to China lies in the fact that it neutralizes any forces, Nationalist Chinese or Western or the two in combination, which might otherwise become hostile to the Peking regime. Up to this stage the Communists have been equal to the task of overthrowing the Kuomintang. But the infant regime, while healthy and hearty, needs outside help before it can fulfill its aspirations to robust manhood. That outside help is now provided by the alliance, pledging Russian military assistance if China should be attacked or threatened with attack. To illustrate it more graphically, the alliance makes an invasion by General Chiang Kai-shek, from his island base of Formosa, virtually impossible except at the risk of a major world war. Furthermore, the alliance has brought economic assistance for China's reconstruction. Though it is on a somewhat limited scale, yet by focusing the Soviet aid on key defense industries and by supplementing it with China's own capital resources, a healthy start is assured for China's industrialization. Thus the alliance extends a protective shield over the new regime so that it can be launched firmly on its road to greater power and strength.

As far as Russia is concerned, the usefulness of the alliance lies in her interest in a new power balance in Asia. In cementing this alliance, Moscow clearly sees the possibilities of using a strong China to counterbalance the United States and Japan in the power structure of the Far East. It is significant that the agreement on Port Arthur declares that in the event of "aggression on the part of Japan or any state which should unite with Japan," China and Russia may "jointly use the naval base of Port Arthur in the interests of conducting joint military operations against the aggressor." The direction of Soviet interest in the conclusion of the treaty is unmistakable. Ever since the end of the nineteenth century, Russia's greatest concern in the Far East has been Japan. Today it still is Japan, or the United States in combination with Japan. The treaty with China is, in a sense, Russia's new investment against the repetition of past history.

Viewed from this angle, then, Russia's attitude toward China does not necessarily point to the desire for a weak China. The prevalent view, prevalent especially during the Korean war, that Russia maneuvered to involve China and the United States in a prolonged conflict so that both would exhaust themselves, is only partly true. No doubt Russia would like to see the United States weakened through the instrumentality of China. But China could hardly accomplish that purpose unless she were reasonably strong. To weaken China, therefore, can hardly be Russia's aim. Russia is sending arms and aid to keep China tolerably strong, so that this strength can be turned to Russia's own advantage. Thus China would be enabled to do the work for Russia in the Far East, leaving Russia free to act in Europe. If China were to become weak, then the Western powers could once again wield a predominant influence over her; Russia would find herself caught in an unstable power balance; and, above all, she would not have a free hand either in the Far East or in Europe. The continued existence of a strong China, pursuing a policy of cooperation with Russia, would be a great boon to the triumph of Russian foreign policy on a global scale.

Now we must turn to the spring of 1950, the months following the conclusion of the Sino-Soviet Alliance. Immediately following publication, the alliance set momentous events going. The cardinal fact that one should bear in mind in approaching this period is that the alliance was launched not only for defensive but for offensive purposes. The question of secret codicils or of secret understandings between Mao and Stalin cannot be solved so long as the necessary evidence is withheld from public knowledge. On the basis of subsequent developments, however, one can reconstruct the grand strategy of the parties to this alliance in the spring of 1950. In brief, the plan of action was a joint Sino-Soviet scheme to take Korea and Formosa and to crown the operation by an attempt to win over Japan. As a flanking move, pressure was also to be put on Indo-China in order to hasten the defeat of the French. But this latter was admittedly secondary in importance. The main objective was an offensive intended to undermine American prestige in Asia by using Korea and Formosa in an initial thrust, after which the major effort was to be directed to the weakening of the collaboration between the United States and Japan.

The two partners allowed themselves and their North Korean protégé about four months (February through June 1950) to prepare for the offensive. The policy calculations of Peking and Moscow during this period were of considerable significance. The method they chose for the realization of their plan was no less than the naked use of force. The pooling of the resources of China, Russia, and North Korea appeared almost invincible. Above all, there was the confident expectation that the United States would not resist their advance with force. The demobilization of the American forces, the general unwillingness of the

American people to be involved in war, and the wavering public opinion among her allies were considered factors that would deter the United States from defensive action. With these major premises in mind, the Soviet and Chinese leaders evolved a plan that embraced both the division of labor and the co-ordination of effort. The offensive was to be carried out in parallel prongs: the North Koreans under Soviet direction would invade South Korea, while the Chinese would attack Formosa. The outcome of this plan was expected to bring simultaneous victory and delimit different spheres of influence—the Russians in Korea and the Chinese in Formosa.

Throughout these months, Communist China carried out her tremendous military build-up in the coastal provinces of Chekiang and Fukien. No less than eighteen Communist armies were concentrated in this area opposite Formosa across the hundred-mile strait. Preparations for crossing the strait were pushed at feverish speed; all kinds of coastal craft were assembled, and training for amphibious operations was intensive. Old airfields were enlarged and new ones built to round out the plans for the impending assault on the island stronghold. By the middle of June the grand partners were ready to strike. During this period, it must be recalled, there was only the usual anti-American propaganda from Peking, but none of the bitter hatred that was manifested after the entry of the United States forces into the Korean war during the last week of June. At the same time the war of the Vietminh against the French in Indo-China was kept only at medium intensity. The explanation is that the Sino-Soviet plan for the main offensive was proceeding according to schedule.

To the great consternation of Peking and Moscow, how-

ever, the very opening shot of the offensive brought instant
retaliation from the United States. If June 25 marked a
moment of triumph for the Communist world, the sudden
turn of the tide certainly made June 27 the blackest day
for the Peking-Moscow axis. In response to a United Nations request to help enforce its demand that the North
Koreans halt their crossing of the 38th parallel, President
Truman ordered American forces under General Mac-
Arthur to aid South Korea. At the same time, the United
States 7th Fleet was dispatched to guard the Formosa Strait
against Communist aggression as well as any possible Kuomintang attack against mainland China. This sensational
development must have been shocking news to the signatories of the Sino-Soviet Alliance. The first and foremost
outcome of President Truman's action was the destruction
of the fundamental premise underlying Communist strategy: namely, that the United States would not resist force
with force. Stemming from the failure of this fundamental
premise came a great procession of events that crowded the
years 1951–4 with a unique record of the bitter clash between the might of the Sino-Soviet Alliance and the
strength of the United States.

It would be an error to say that the Sino-Soviet Alliance
was weakened by the United States entry into the Korean
war. What actually happened was that the resistance offered by the United States brought the Communist aggression to a standstill, while the determination of the Peking-
Moscow axis to maintain its line only served to deepen its
hatred of the United States. The manner in which the
Communist plan of action was upset by this American resistance forms most interesting study. In the first place,
confronted by the military power of the United States and

her allies in Korea, the path of Communist expansion could no longer be the easy one originally expected. It soon became evident to the Peking-Moscow axis that their hopes of taking Korea were not to be realized, while their plan to draw Japan into their orbit had to be entirely abandoned for the moment. In fact, the one and only concern of the Communist partners was to hold their ground in North Korea under the fire of the United Nations forces. In the second place, the stationing of the United States 7th Fleet in the Formosan waters dashed the hopes of the giant Communist armada waiting in Chekiang and Fukien provinces to take Formosa. In the third place, to avoid a Communist debacle in Korea, Communist China was virtually compelled to shift her forces to the northern theater. The entry of massive numbers of Chinese troops into the Korean war, made necessary by the retreat of the North Koreans into Manchuria, meant a radical alteration in the Communist plan. The hopes held high on the eve of the offensive that there would be a two-pronged movement against Korea in the north and Formosa in the south were entirely abandoned after November. The long-range significance of this forced change in military strategy is even more noteworthy. With China rather than the North Korean protégé of Russia bearing the brunt of the fighting, the idea of a Russian sphere of influence in Korea had to give way to one of Chinese supremacy in this particular region as in her other peripheral areas.

From this point on, the Korean war meant hard and long-drawn-out fighting. The casualties were of course heavy on both sides. By throwing in virtually hundreds of thousands of troops, the Chinese Communists were prepared to trade untold lives for victory. This was imperative if the morale of the Communist front and the prestige of the Alliance were to be saved. None the less, new and unforeseen trends were developing behind the scenes. Soviet Russia took on the burden of rushing in huge quantities of military supplies to keep the Chinese armies going. Of necessity, Soviet Russia and her North Korean protégé receded more or less into the background, leaving China the dominant figure in Korea. This development lasted from November 1950 till July 1951 when it was finally decided that there was nothing further to be gained on the battlefield and that truce talks would be advisable.

No less than two full years intervened from the time the Soviet delegate proposed a truce at the United Nations till the actual signing of the Korean armistice. The reason for such apparent Communist intransigence and procrastination is not far to seek. With their aggression checked, the Soviet and Chinese partners needed all this time to revamp their strategy. In the end, they could not reactivate their offensive against Korea and Formosa. The armistice was signed in July 1953, leaving the Korean struggle deadlocked at the halfway point and the Formosa struggle hardly carried beyond the agitation stage. For possible future exploitation, however, a bitter campaign of hatred against the United States was stepped up inside China. Down to this present day, Peking maintains the adamant position that the United States, in coming to the defense of South Korea, acted the part of an "imperialist aggressor" and that any settlement in Korea must be on terms advocated by China.

It was only as a "second best" during the protracted negotiations for the Korean truce that Peking took up the Indo-China issue. As has been said above, in the original strategy mapped out in the spring of 1950 by Peking and Moscow, Indo-China was intended only as a flanking move and was not considered particularly urgent. In view of the changed circumstances following the turn of events in Korea, a sudden shift of emphasis was placed on Indo-China. The Vietminh forces based in the northwestern corner of the country were encouraged to mount new and larger offensives against the French. The Chinese did not actually have to fight alongside the Vietminh, because here, unlike Korea, there was no involvement of the United Nations. But large quantities of artillery, ammunition, and equipment came from Communist China across the border to strengthen the Vietminh. Secretary Dulles, in detailing some of the aid sent by China, indicated that a ranking military representative from Communist China was stationed at the headquarters of the Communist Commander-in-Chief in Indo-China; Chinese technical advisers were attached to the divisional headquarters in the field; a considerable number of anti-aircraft guns, radar-controlled, at Dien Bien Phu were operated by Chinese gunners to bring down French aircraft; about a thousand supply trucks supported the Vietminh forces in the siege of Dien Bien Phu. If it were not for these supplies, it is doubtful whether the fate of Dien Bien Phu, the important bastion blocking the rebel route to the Red River delta, would have been decided so speedily in favor of the Vietminh.

As things turned out, however, Chinese Communist aid to the Vietminh brought a tremendous victory. The French and the Vietnamese forces were unable to withstand further pressure from the Vietminh. The Paris government and the European allies were all anxious for peace at almost any price. At the Geneva Conference (April–June

1954) the Peking-Moscow axis gained a resounding victory, which went a long way to redeem the setbacks it had received in Korea. It is illuminating to note that neither Chou nor Molotov made any attempt to conceal their hands in the Indo-China struggle. The duet played by them at Geneva was a living reproduction of Article IV of the Sino-Soviet Treaty of 1950. The Vietminh representatives remained in the background, while Chou and Molotov consulted each other on all "problems affecting the common interests of the Soviet Union and China" and openly acted as arbiters for the Communist side. In their speeches pointed references were made to the loss of prestige sustained by the United States, while the parties directly concerned (the Vietnam and France) were acclaimed for their sagacity in yielding to the Communist pressure. From the standpoint of the fortunes of the Sino-Soviet Alliance, the Geneva settlement of the Indo-China struggle certainly furnished some comic relief to the tragic climax of Korea.

Before we proceed to examine the next stage of Peking's foreign relations, it is useful to say a few more words about the Korean war in its broad historical perspective. Following Chinese entry into the Korean war, in November 1950, certain students of history advanced the thesis that Peking's action represented a reassertion of China's traditional interest in her "border dependencies." This view is not entirely accurate. From the T'ang to our own time, every major intervention in Korea by either China or Russia was caused by rivalry with Japan rather than by a mere desire to regain a "border dependency." The T'ang conquest of Korea was carried out in order to beat off the first Japanese intervention in history. Under the Ming dynasty, a long war was again fought against Japan over Korea, ending in the defeat of the Japanese and the re-establishment of a Chinese protectorate. In more recent times two major Korean wars were fought within the decade 1894–1905. The first arose out of the clash of Chinese and Japanese interests; the second, out of the clash of Russian and Japanese interests. Both ended in the victory of Japan.

The latest Korean war was not at all different in its essential setting. What inspired the war was the ambition of Soviet Russia and Communist China to eliminate the influence of Japan and together with that the dominance of the United States. Once again the conflict was a struggle arising from international rivalry and not from a determination on China's part to recover a lost "border dependency." What made this latest war different from previous hostilities over Korea was the fact that its outcome was not a victory for the Chinese side, as with the T'ang and Ming expeditions, nor did it favor the Japanese or, in this instance, the American side, as was true of the Sino-Japanese and the Russo-Japanese wars. The war, stalemated and only terminated by an uneasy armistice, is in reality unfinished business. As I have said before, the Communist position remains adamant, while at the same time one may take for granted that the United States has no intention either of giving way. In this sense, then, the political outlook for a "lasting peace" in Korea remains as dim as in 1950–1.

The events in Indo-China, on the other hand, seem to have run truer to the historical pattern. Throughout the long centuries of Chinese history, Indo-China (especially the northern part) was intimately bound up with China economically, strategically, and culturally. Indo-China was never a source of invasions but rather the recipient of strong Chinese migrations and strong Chinese cultural influences. Thus from the Han dynasty on, there were long periods when Annam was a vassal state of China. In the latter half of the nineteenth century, as the result of a war fought with France, China was led by unfortunate circumstances to renounce her authority over Indo-China in favor of France. Some eighty years intervened during which China, caught in a welter of weakness and chaos, had to accept the loss of this protectorate to France. But by the end of World War II, the moral and material strength of French rule had all but spent its force. The emergence of the Vietminh, a movement not unlike the rise of the Chinese Communists against the Kuomintang, presented the opportunity for Peking to reassert China's interest in this particular frontier area. As in the past, Peking's policy was to give aid to those favored and to help them wrest power from the French and the Vietnamese.

As far as China's interests are concerned, the outcome of the Indo-China struggle has been a great success. This was largely so because it represented a different kind of struggle from that in Korea. Here, as we have seen, Communist China did not engage in open military intervention in a major international conflict, but aided the fight of a native revolutionary movement against the rule of the French. In the process, Ho Chi-minh and the Vietminh turned to Peking for moral as well as material support. As a result, Peking can rest assured not only of a secure southern frontier but also of an implicit overlordship in Tonking. Whatever aspirations China may have entertained of reviving the old relationship, between the Empire and the vassal state are being satisfactorily fulfilled. There is little doubt that the future outlook is favorable to the Communists.

The Vietminh stands an excellent chance of further extending its influence southward—a prospect hardly comparable to the situation created by Syngman Rhee's stubborn resistance in South Korea.

But the Geneva Conference, successful as it was for the Communists, really marked a turning-point in the evolution of the foreign relations of Communist China. Up to the spring of 1954, Peking pursued a course of aggressive expansion, but her offensive was checked by the United States in Korea. The Communist victory in Indo-China indeed restored some of Peking's lost prestige, but behind the surface of victory it was clear that the giant offensive as originally conceived had hit a stone wall. Accordingly, after the Geneva Conference, Communist China adopted a change in method. The concept of military aggression had to be shelved. In its place a new approach was instituted. This approach comprised two parallel phases, each conceived with great boldness and ingenuity and closely related to the other. One phase was to cultivate the friendship of the Asian nations with a view to building up a considerable following in Asia that would strengthen China's defiance of the United States. The other phase was to maintain tension at a high pitch, hoping thereby to force the United States to make concessions. Thus this stage of Peking's policy, while abandoning actual aggression, was essentially similar in spirit to those which preceded it, inasmuch as the basic concept remained unchanged: to seek great-power status through coercion rather than through negotiation.

Let us first examine Peking's campaign to win Asian hegemony. By upholding the slogan of "peaceful coexistence," Peking bent most of her diplomatic effort during the one-year period from the Geneva Conference in the spring of 1954 to the Bandung Conference in the spring of 1955 on building up an Asian bloc, which she wished to use as a weapon in a giant political offensive against the United States. Geographically, this ambitious bid for Asian hegemony encompassed the lands extending from the Persian Gulf around the Indian Ocean and the South Seas to the Sea of Japan. It is to be recalled that when the Indo-China war reached the point where it was practically won by the Communists, the United States took the lead in forming the Southeast Asia Treaty Organization (SEATO) in order to draw the Asian nations into a defensive alliance against further Communist aggression. As this movement gathered momentum, Communist China immediately embarked upon her new policy of peaceful coexistence to woo these nations away from the United States. The target of Peking's new line embraced Pakistan, India, Ceylon, Burma, Thailand, Indonesia, the Philippines, and Japan. She particularly focused her attention on such neutralist states as India and Burma, which had no interest in aligning themselves with the United States in the cold war. In April 1954, five basic principles representing China's offer of peaceful coexistence made their first public appearance in an agreement negotiated with India relative to trade and travel in Tibet. These principles, later reiterated in negotiations with other Asian nations, were: respect for each other's territorial integrity and sovereignty; nonaggression; noninterference in each other's internal affairs; equality and mutual benefit; and peaceful coexistence. This marked a clear bid on Peking's part to win the nations of Asia by making explicit her peaceful intentions and desire for co-operation.

To strengthen the friendly gesture, Chou En-lai, on his way back from Geneva in June 1954, visited the capitals of India and Burma and held cordial conferences with their leaders, Nehru and U Nu. The result of such efforts on the part of Peking became obvious in September. When the Manila Pact was signed and the Southeast Asia Treaty Organization (SEATO) formally established, only Pakistan, Thailand, and the Philippines among the Asian nations participated as signatories, the other five signatories being the United States, Great Britain, France, Australia, and New Zealand. The great majority of the Asian nations stayed away. Thus, from Peking's standpoint, the first phase of the application of her new policy of peaceful coexistence seemed to have borne fruit.

The action of the Communist leaders of Peking in pursuing this policy conjures up in one's mind the grandiose scheme of Cheng Ho of the Ming dynasty, some five hundred years ago, to establish Chinese hegemony over this same vast area. Yet the difference in the political backgrounds of the two seemingly analogous situations can hardly be overemphasized. Cheng Ho's journey was presumably inspired by a desire to locate a pretender to the throne, while his ambition was to assert Ming prowess and to exact tribute from prospective vassals. The mission of Chou En-lai, far from asking for tribute, carried the offer of coexistence. The deeper objective underlying this sweet and reasonable exterior, however, was to win the support of a giant regional bloc in an international power struggle of the first magnitude. The undermining, if not the elimination, of the influence of the United States in Asia was the big stake for which Communist China played in this period.

Accordingly, a reckless political offensive against the United States paralleled Peking's effort to acquire Asian hegemony. *Tension* was the word that epitomized the spirit of this aspect of Communist policy. No other word obtained greater currency or plagued men's minds more corrosively. A variety of tactical concepts, for the most part foreign to the Western mentality, were set in motion by Peking in this political offensive. In the first place, Peking played up a war scare. Knowing that the Western powers were tired of war, Peking exploited every possible advantage by concentrating on the implicit threat of her military build-up. Warmongering, so characteristic of upstart and power-hungry tyrants, was Peking's number-one card.

In the second place, the Communist technique of guerrilla warfare was applied to diplomacy. The motto of the Communists on the battlefield has always been: "When the enemy advances, we retreat. When he retreats, we pursue. When he is tired, we attack." This motto now became the guiding principle of Peking's diplomatic moves. When the West wished to negotiate, Peking stalled. When the West stood firm, she retreated or softened her tone. Peking's intransigence was as astounding as it was ubiquitous. By the same token, when other nations accused her of expansionism, Peking immediately threw charges at the United States, blaming her for trying to sabotage the "people's democracy" and thereby putting China in the class of victims of American "aggression."

In the third place, the Communists made a mockery of the concept of international negotiation. They regarded the conference table not as a meeting-ground for give and take, or for demand and compromise, but rather as a continuation of the battlefield. They did not attend conferences in order to settle matters, but to reiterate their demands in an effort to obtain a wider hearing or to reconnoiter and size up the opponent in preparation for the next move against him.

Finally, the Communists proved themselves great masters of an endless alternation of methods. Their propaganda created a smoke screen in order to confound the opponent, while the basic objective remained fixed. The Communists also relied heavily on patience in adversity. They never moved with impetuosity. Knowing that the American temperament was much less able to endure the long-drawn-out uncertainty of what the future held, they sought to wear down their opponent by attrition.

It was under the cover of these tactics that Peking carried on her war of nerves against the United States in the period under consideration (1954–5), at times stretching the peace in Asia almost to the breaking-point. There were a number of issues over which Peking's interests clashed with those of the United States. Wherever she could extort the greater advantage, there Peking directed her major attention. Wherever the advantages were less clear, she relegated the issues to a secondary place. Thus on the Korean question China's attitude was to leave it at stalemate. At the Geneva Conference her representatives made it clear that unless agreement was reached on her terms, there would be no political settlement. In other words, she was biding her time and preferred to leave the matter deadlocked. This was an issue on which China found it relatively difficult to arouse sympathetic hearing, and consequently it was unprofitable as a weapon in advancing her political offensive.

Similarly, though China was most anxious to undermine

Japan's ties with the United States, her approach to the
problem was one of slow advance through economic in-
ducements. During 1953, after much publicity was given
to the repatriation of Japanese nationals, Peking initiated
a campaign to woo Japanese businessmen by proffering a
lucrative China trade as bait. As postwar restrictions set
up by the United States seriously hampered the Japanese
economy, Peking seized upon this to drive her wedge between Japan and the United States. Unofficial trade mis-
sions were exchanged between China and Japan, and a
number of barter agreements signed. The fact that the
same old colonial pattern of trade, under which Japan sold
tremendous quantities of cheap consumer goods to China
and imported from her large volumes of industrial raw
materials, could not be repeated under the new regime in
China, was deliberately ignored. Meantime, Peking offered Japan a nonaggression pact if she would break away
from the United States. In the autumn of 1954 Russia and
China made a joint bid for the normalization of relations
with Japan, expressing the hope that the Japanese people
would find the strength to free themselves from the "semi-
colonial status" imposed by the United States. In the course
of 1955, further statements were exchanged between Moscow and Tokyo on the desirability of establishing normal
relations between themselves and between Peking and
Tokyo. These overtures to Japan, however, did not represent China's main drive against the United States, for on
this, as on the Korean issue, Peking realized that she could
not count upon Asian support of her cause.

It was on the question of the admission of Communist
China into the United Nations and on the Formosa issue
that Peking staged her most virulent political offensive

against the United States. For here were two questions over which Communist China could arouse tremendous sympathy among the Asian nations and could create disharmony between the United States on the one hand and the Asian nations and many of America's allies on the other. The agitation over Peking's entry into the United Nations during this period forms a most interesting case study of her strategy to heighten tension. That Communist China wanted ultimately to win admission into the United Nations and thus establish her big-power status is beyond question. But, contrary to the opinion of many, it is doubtful whether, at the time, she seriously entertained any hope of being admitted. Statements from Peking breathed open defiance and denunciation. Whenever the leaders of the regime came into contact with the United Nations, they chose to disparage the international body instead of treating with it. Rather than seek admission in the customary way, Peking's accent was on attacking the United States' opposition to her admission. Her main interest at the time was to exaggerate the impression that she was being ill-used by the United States and to arouse anti-American sentiment among the Asian nations and among the allies of the United States. To a considerable extent Peking believed that such efforts could be successful, especially as she watched the reactions of Great Britain and India, which appeared more exercised about her nonadmission than she was herself.

Even more explosive was Peking's campaign against the United States over the Formosa issue. Peking's bitterness against the United States had deepened ever since she had lost her one and only chance of capturing Formosa when the United States 7th Fleet undertook to defend it. In

spite of this, it was clear that Peking would hardly dare to
venture a major war with the United States. First, she was
not equal to such an undertaking. Second, it is doubtful
whether Moscow would favor so dangerous an involvement
by her partner. Yet Peking repeatedly asserted her claim
that Formosa was a domestic issue, and that the United
States was interfering in the Chinese civil war. The idea
that the final disposition of the island had to await the
action of the signatories of the peace treaty with Japan
and that until then this was an international issue was
entirely ignored by the Communists. There is no question
that there was considerable validity in the Communist
position, inasmuch as civil war still existed between the
Communist and Nationalist governments, and Peking's
desire to "liberate" Formosa was understandable. On the
other hand, the American position had its point, which
was not to be discounted. These conflicting claims were
further complicated by the fact that the Nationalist government was the only Chinese government recognized and
supported by the United States. The result of these unrelenting views and positions was the emergence of two *de
facto* Chinese governments, one on the mainland and one
on Formosa. Since neither party would or could retreat
from its position, the Formosa question had for the time
become well-nigh insoluble.

This was the crux of the issue, which Peking seized upon
as a basis for her strategy against the United States. So long
as the Formosa situation was insoluble, Peking used it to
poison international relations in the Far East. Throughout
1954 and the early months of 1955 Peking kept her agitation over the Formosa question in high gear. At times
her military build-up on the Fukien coast threatened an

impending outbreak of hostilities. At others, the tension appeared to decrease. Upon the signing of the Manila Pact and the formal establishment of SEATO, however, the war of nerves entered an acute stage. Peking threatened to begin her liberation of Formosa by taking the offshore islands which were held by the forces of the Nationalist government on Formosa. Meantime, the news came that, in an act of virtual blackmail against the United States and in violation of international law, Peking had imprisoned a number of American airmen who were taken captive during the Korean war.

At no other time were Communist China and the United States closer to a fresh outbreak of hostilities than in the winter months of 1954–5. While the world hoped anxiously for a solution of the question of the imprisoned airmen through the visit of the Secretary-General of the United Nations to Peking, China endeavored again to force the retreat of the United States from Formosa. When the United Nations Security Council invited Peking to send a representative to discuss a cease-fire proposal, the Communists refused to attend except at the price of excluding the Nationalists and obtaining their seat in the Council. As was to be expected, this demand came to nothing. A few days later, Russian Foreign Minister Molotov suggested calling a ten-power conference either in Shanghai or in New Delhi to discuss the Formosa question. Again the condition was the exclusion of Nationalist China from the talks, and again the United States held out in firm opposition. In the meantime the United States Congress adopted a resolution empowering the President to act as he deemed necessary for the defense of Formosa and the Pescadores.

This reaffirmation of the determination of the United

States to defend Formosa added a finality to her stand against Communist agitation. In the months immediately following, the Communists succeeded in getting possession of the Tachen group of islands to the northwest of Formosa following the planned evacuation of Nationalist garrisons. But the threat to take the Matsu and Quemoy groups, due west of Formosa across the Strait, was not carried out. At this point it undoubtedly became evident to Peking that her policy of seeking political conquest through defiance and provocation had perhaps reached the limit of safety. Should she continue in the same direction, she would either run the risk of a major war or effect her own isolation. In either case, it would block her ambition to play the leading role in Asia.

The significance of Peking's highhanded act in the imprisonment of the American fliers was more far-reaching than was generally realized at the time. The issue was ready-made to stir deep resentment among the American people. The indignation thus aroused led to a hardening of the American attitude toward the entire behavior of Peking, leaving the advocates of patience and understanding without an argument. The public was, of course, denied knowledge of what exactly transpired during the visit of the Secretary-General of the United Nations to Peking in connection with this issue. Yet it was clear that the mission was not a failure. This was the first indication that Peking, too, was beginning an "agonizing reappraisal" of her strategy.

In such a reappraisal, the prospects of her hegemony over the Asian nations no doubt weighed heavily in the thinking of Communist China. Up to this point, her effort to enlist the sympathy of the Asian nations in support of her

opposition to the United States had been largely successful. It now appeared, however, that the enthusiasm of the
neutralist nations had already reached its peak. In view
of the determined stand of the United States, would the
Asian nations rally behind China if she continued to
foment tension? If Asian hegemony were to be used as a
weapon against the United States, would not sympathy
eventually give way to skepticism over Peking's ultimate
motives? These were among the crucial questions that beset
the Communist leaders while they sought to evaluate their
tactics.

As Peking considered the prospects of her bid for Asian
hegemony, she no doubt found that her assets and liabilities offset one another. In her favor were two factors of
strength. For one thing, she could use to good advantage
the existence of nationalism and economic underdevelopment in the Asian nations. The success of China's Revolution gave her a natural right to leadership. Sun Yat-sen, in
his will, exhorted the Chinese to enlist the help of other
oppressed peoples so that the Chinese Revolution would
live on to success. This the Communist leaders in Peking
found to be no longer necessary. China's Revolution had
actually forged so far ahead of the struggling movements in
the rest of Asia that the new China was in a strong position
to awaken and lead the other peoples. This was something neither Sun nor most of his contemporaries dared
dream of.

Another element of strength in the Communist approach
was its stress on peaceful coexistence. Whatever Peking's
ultimate intentions might be, her appeal for co-operation
and good-neighborliness put her program in quite a different light from, for instance, the Pan-Asianism of pre-

war Japan. Unlike the experience with Japan, whose rise
to power in East Asia in the late nineteenth and early twentieth centuries led to outright territorial conquests, the
influence of the hegemony sought by Communist China
would be felt in her leadership of the Asian nations against
the vestiges of Western imperialism. Japan joined the
ranks of the imperialist powers and exploited her neighbors. Communist China, on the other hand, posed as the
champion of her weak and underdeveloped neighbors
against these very imperialist powers. Thus the Asian nations, in spite of all that reason could disallow, found themselves subtly drawn to the line of their great neighbor not
only by the promise of peace but by their admiration of
her own success. The way of Japan's Pan-Asianism was
"yi li fu jen" ("to seek assent by the use of force") —a
course that the Communists knew could not succeed. The
Confucian way was *"ye te fu jen"* ("to seek assent by the
practice of virtue") —a code of conduct to which the Communists were hardly equal. But in the twilight zone between force and virtue, the Communists knew that they
could find a way to establish their ascendancy, an ascendancy much more effective as a weapon in international
rivalry than that attempted by Japan with her Pan-
Asianism.

Nevertheless, other forces militated against the interests
of Peking. The Sino-Soviet Alliance, designed by its archi-
tects for aggression, was actually a source of misgiving
among the nations yearning for emancipation. In that
sense, it was a hindrance to the policy of winning Asian
friends. Moreover, while Peking's psychological and propaganda war against the United States had won a sympathetic hearing among the Asian nations, this advantage

could have only a limited duration. For as those nations stabilized themselves, the distorted picture of the United States as the "aggressor" would inevitably lose its appeal. *"Hsui lao shih ch'u"* ("The rock is bound to emerge as the tide subsides"). Herein was the basic weakness of Peking's strategy to rally Asia against the United States. Like all *"li chien chi"* ("alienation plots") in history, time was the deadly enemy. True, the leaders of the Asian nations were jealous of yielding too much to the influence of the United States; but they also took a dim view of the long-range effects of Peking's bid for hegemony. They were fully aware that today's talk of Asian brotherhood and unity could easily transform itself into a new imperialism tomorrow.

Such was the balance sheet of China's assets and liabilities when the Afro-Asian nations prepared for the convening of the Bandung Conference in April 1955. It is of some interest to note that participation in the conference was actively sought by Communist China herself. She had reached a turning-point in her play for international status. To intensify her provocation of the United States or to disengage herself from the isolation of her own creation—this was the burning question to which Peking was eager to find the answer. As Chou En-lai emplaned for the Indonesian conference, his purpose was not to dominate the conference, but rather to determine the attitudes of the participating nations toward China. With this as a basis of judgment, he would be enabled to shape the next phase in Peking's strategy.

What Chou En-lai discovered at Bandung was at once instructive and startling. Far from forming a grand coalition against the alleged imperialism of the United States, the twenty-nine nations participating in the conference revealed marked cleavages on this question. China and the Vietminh, of course, formed the Communist bloc. The other twenty-seven nations were divided between the neutralist group led by India, Burma, and Indonesia and the pro-Western group led by Turkey, Pakistan, and the Philippines. The neutralist states were sympathetic to Peking, and it was confidently expected that they would set the tone of the conference. But no sooner had the conference opened than it became clear that Nehru and U Nu were unable to steer the discussions along the course they advocated. The strength of the pro-Western group was a revelation to both the conferees and the outside world. Statements by the leaders of Turkey, Iran, Iraq, Pakistan, Thailand, and the Philippines spoke eloquently in defense of the United States foreign policy and in condemnation of the much greater terror of Communist expansion and subversion, of "a new super-barbarism, a new super-imperialism, and a new super-power," as Brigadier General Carlos P. Romulo put it. Even more surprising and consequently more effective was the voice of Ceylon, for she parted company with India and Burma by denouncing the threat of Communism. Her Premier, Sir John Kotelawala, sharply attacked the new colonialism of Soviet Russia and Communist China. In the discussion on dependent peoples, Sir John charged that Communist policies, if unchecked, would reduce the free nations of Europe and Asia to satellites of Russia and China, and demanded that China as a reassuring gesture call upon Communist groups in Asia and Africa to disband.

The week-long deliberations disclosed that almost without exception the nations attending the conference hated

power blocs of any sort. They wanted to end, not to pro-
long, the cold war. They made it clear that peace was their
paramount objective, and any plan that ran counter to
the interests of peace would be condemned by them. The
impact of these sentiments convinced Chou En-lai of a
number of things. First, in view of the serious distrust of
China's motives entertained by these Asian nations, the
realization of an anti-American Asian bloc would be extremely difficult. Second, further exploitation of the strategy of heightening tension against the United States might
not only deny her the continued support of her Asian
neighbors but even cause a fatal split in Asian ranks.
Third, Chou began to realize that the time had probably
come to take steps to avoid isolation, to open new avenues
for maneuvering rather than to drift into a position of
weakness under an inflexible policy. Fourth, if China
hoped that India and Burma would continue to play an
effective role as neutralist nations in support of her views,
she had no choice but to initiate a newer policy that would
buttress their efforts to mediate between her and the
United States.

Influenced by these considerations, Chou assured the
conference that his desire was to be conciliatory, that the
Chinese delegation wanted "to seek common ground and
not to create divergence." He side-stepped frontal clashes
with delegates protesting the new imperialism of Communist China, but worked quietly and patiently to gain
popularity, to extend the area of contact with each of the
states, and to inspire trust in China's peaceful intentions.
Before the conference ended, Chou made a number of significant moves designed to steer China's foreign policy
away from its usual unqualified offensive against the

United States to a role urging negotiation. On the Formosa question, for instance, Chou declared that China was
ready to enter into bilateral negotiations with the United
States. He refrained from angry debate on the denunciation of Communist expansionism by Pakistan and Ceylon.
He agreed to the Ten Principles drawn up by the conference. Before leaving Bandung, he invited Thailand and
Cambodia to send representatives to make an on-the-spot
check in South China and thus assure themselves that there
were no preparations for the invasion of their borders.
Most significant of all, as a first step in meeting the issue
of subversion by overseas Chinese in the Southeast Asian
countries, Chou signed a treaty with Indonesia, providing
that the Chinese resident there would be required to decide within two years whether they wanted Chinese or
Indonesian nationality.

It would be inaccurate to say that one week's observation
of the climate at Bandung could bring about a complete
change of mind in Chou. The truth was that Bandung did
not cause a change in the goals of Peking at all, but it did
inspire a shift in tactics on her part. Ever since the clari-
fication of the United States stand on Formosa, Peking
had had serious misgivings about her own techniques. The
unmistakable signs at Bandung helped to bring about a
decisive reversal in Peking's diplomatic strategy. Display-
ing the same flexibility that had been characteristic of the
Communist leaders throughout the years, Chou moved
quickly with his offer to negotiate with the United States.
In doing so, he showed both courage and foresight, for he
succeeded in taking the initiative once again into his hands
just as China was on the verge of losing her great diplomatic battle.

Peking's diplomatic adroitness became clear only a few months after Bandung when her call for bilateral talks with the United States was made a reality. Thanks to the efforts of Nehru and his aides in the various world chancelleries, coupled with their entreaties for relaxing tension, the way was cleared to inaugurate a new pattern of dealing with the United States. With dramatic suddenness, the release of the imprisoned American fliers raised the curtain in Geneva for the first of what promised to be a long series of direct talks between Communist China and the United States. In this new phase, the erstwhile war of nerves had not as yet been disclaimed. It was only relegated to the background. What constituted a great victory for Peking's diplomatic strategy, however, was the fact that she had successfully veered away from a mounting impasse and had opened up boundless vistas for fresh maneuvering and bargaining.

In this new phase of direct talks with the United States, Communist China was evidently prepared to abandon or greatly curtail the use of her old strategy of heightening tension. She had called a halt in her warmongering and anti-American vituperation. If she had not entirely given up the technique of wearing out her opponent, she certainly was holding her guerrilla diplomacy to a minimum. This was the price that China was willing to pay in order to keep the direct talks going.

As far as her objectives were concerned, Peking's greatest need was to break through her isolation. Her past methods had to a considerable degree set her apart from normal association with other nations. It was strange indeed for the aspiring leader in Asia to find herself confronted by SEATO and the mutual-security treaty between the United States and Chiang, quarantined by a trade embargo imposed by the Western nations, and above all barred from membership in the United Nations. It became of paramount importance at this point for Peking to move into the ranks of the majority, for only by so doing could she extricate herself from a position of weakness and operate from a new position of strength.

Only in the light of this basic aim can one understand Peking's change of front. First of all, she set herself to undermine or destroy all regional organizations (SEATO, for instance) from which she had been excluded and which were consequently aimed at her. A cardinal condition in the new regional system proposed by Peking was the inclusion of both China and the United States as members, for this would enable China to utilize that degree of leverage among the Asian nations which her power warranted. Moreover, with her internal needs expanding constantly, China had to break through the trade embargo of the Western nations and lift the trade barriers between herself and Japan. The limited quantities of Soviet aid and the one-sided direction of China's foreign trade were not designed to develop her internal strength to a degree commensurate with her ambition to join the ranks of the great powers. In the economic field, then, as in the political, China had definite objectives to pursue.

Peking's greatest interest, however, still lay in resolving the questions of Formosa and of her admission into the United Nations. Up to this phase of development, as we have seen, Peking pressed for solutions by attacking American involvement in Formosa and American opposition to her United Nations membership. The old strategy, however, had yielded neither Formosa nor acceptance into the family of nations. Peking found herself constrained then to turn to the more generally accepted mode of international negotiation for the satisfaction of these same demands. In this way she could more effectively press her claim to United Nations membership and ultimately request action by the international organization on the question of Formosa. At the same time she could tackle the problem of diplomatic recognition by the United States.

Viewed in this light, the shift in Peking's diplomacy was significant. It cleared the poisoned atmosphere of the first five years of Communist China's dealings with the West and introduced a new climate for future battles. It is important to remember, however, that despite Peking's change of method, there was no change in her aims. In fact, it was her expectation that the new approach would yield returns and achieve her ends more advantageously. Once direct talks were under way, one step would lead to another. Meetings between China and the United States, begun at lower diplomatic levels, would eventually be climaxed by conferences between their top representatives. The foreign relations of China, then, had reached a new and crucial stage. As far as the West was concerned, China's change of approach offered a challenge greater than ever, for unlike the era of Communist aggression and propaganda warfare, the new era of negotiation compelled the West not to resist but to probe, to answer, and to devise solutions. As far as China was concerned, under the new strategy she appeared to stand a good chance of winning what she had failed to get otherwise.

V

THE PROBLEMS OF RECONSTRUCTION

❁

THE DEVELOPMENT of the foreign relations of Communist China has presented the picture of a new power engaged in widespread conflict with the Western nations. In such a pursuit she has been following perilous methods and taking zigzag turns. She is determined and belligerent, for she is none too sure about the outcome of her struggle.

The process of China's internal reconstruction, however, presents quite a different prospect. Here, too, China faces many difficult problems. But she has been making remarkable progress. In the brief period of a few years she has demonstrated her ability to marshal her resources, to map out a practical program, and to make a good start on her industrialization. The notable features of her endeavor in this direction are the uninterrupted advance of the program and the unshaken confidence of the leaders. Here powerful influences of permanent importance are laying the foundations of the new China.

The problems of China's internal reconstruction are indeed stupendous. With a population of 580,000,000 and an economy badly underdeveloped, the immensity of the task is easily understood. During the period of subversion the Communists exploited the weakness of the Kuomintang regime with easy advantage: they had the discontent

of the masses on their side. Now in the new era of reconstruction, they face an entirely different challenge. It is
their task to plan, to lead, and to build. They have to bring
stability out of chaos and to create strength and prosperity.
Yet in spite of such odds the Communist leaders appear to
know how to carry their program to success. Their mood
is one of confident expectation.

There is no fixed date that one may consider the start-
ing-point of reconstruction. Certainly it did not begin
abruptly with the end of the Korean war or with the an-
nouncement of the Five-Year Plan. All the basic measures
taken by Peking following the establishment of the new
regime may be considered as preparatory to the central
tasks of economic reconstruction. As discussed in a preceding chapter, the speedy restoration of normal conditions
was one of the factors of Communist strength. It is to the
credit of the Communist leaders that within less than two
years after the inauguration of the new government in
Peking, they accomplished a remarkable recovery of the
nation's economy. By new and swift measures, they restored railway communications that ensured the free movement of food and goods between city and countryside,
thereby ending the crippling dislocations of the last days
of Kuomintang rule. They also brought inflation under
effective control, thus eliminating one of the basic causes
of corruption. The rapid stabilization of prices further
discouraged speculation and hoarding. In a general recovery of confidence and normalcy, the numbers of the
unemployed were greatly curtailed. Meantime, in the field
of public finance Peking moved to abolish all abuses in
taxation, centralized the finances of the civil government
as well as of the armed forces, and virtually balanced the

budget. As though Providence was also on their side, the Communists profited immensely from three successive years of rich harvests from 1950 through 1952. The net result of these developments in the initial years of the regime was to put its economy on a sound footing—something that neither the Taipings nor the Bolsheviks achieved upon their accession to power. Both tried hasty measures of pure communism, only to be rewarded with chaos and deprivation. The Peking government scrupulously avoided such precipitate action. They made it their first job to protect all available resources, to build on peace and order, and to gain an effective mastery of the nation's production and distribution. As a result, these measures obviated many dangers and cleared the deck, so to speak, for more important measures to come.

The years 1949–53 witnessed a series of broad endeavors to increase the stability of the new regime. For one thing, the Communists moved quickly to restore industrial productivity. Coal and iron production in 1952 nearly caught up with the prewar peak level, while steel production in 1952 exceeded that level by thirty per cent. This is a record that stands in striking contrast to the serious drop in production in Soviet Russia during the years 1918–21. Next the government tackled the food problem of the nation with considerable success. Since unification had removed provincial barriers to the flow of grain, and since hoarding and speculation by the merchants had been stopped, Peking was able to pursue a sound program of food distribution and transportation. By using surplus areas to help the deficient sections, the food problem of the country on a nationwide basis was given a rational solution, which obviated many unnecessary crises. State control of the nation's economy indeed increased, but it worked to the benefit of the masses. For, as the government stepped in to claim greater freedom of action, the people's needs met with adequate recognition. Only the greed and profit of the merchants were sacrificed.

Meantime, the Land Reform Law was passed and went into effect in mid-1950. Prior to this, the Communist movement, as we have seen, had been carrying out land reforms in scattered regions under its control. The law of 1950 extended the reform to the entire country. Under the operation of this law, the stupendous task of land redistribution on a nationwide scale was pushed to a successful completion by the end of 1952. This time, party cadres were sent by the government into the tens of thousands of villages to direct the peasant population in taking land away from the landlords and distributing it to the poor and landless peasants. The over-all objective was to abolish the "landownership system of feudal exploitation by the landlord class," tempered somewhat by a moderate treatment of the rich and middle peasants for the sake of upholding production. By redistributing the land taken from the landlords in plots varying from an average holding of 2.7 mou (1 mou $= \frac{1}{6}$ acre) per head in Manchuria to 1.9 mou in North China and 1.3 mou in Central and South China, the enforcement of this law knocked out the landlord class and substantially eased the lot of about sixty per cent of the rural population, who up to this time had owned no land at all or else so little that they could scarcely eke out a living. The economic status of the middle peasants remained about the same as before. But for all the peasants the days of high rent were gone. Varying with the locality, the peasants were now required to pay to the government a tax in kind representing between eighteen and twenty-seven per cent of the yield of their land. Thus the peasants retained a greater share of their produce and were better able to solve the problem of subsistence. This measure providing for land equalization based on the concept of "land to the cultivator" was a capital victory in the government's push toward social transformation. The immediate benefit to Peking was threefold: it won for the government the gratitude and support of the peasantry; the new peasant associations gave Peking an instrument for better rural administration; and it eliminated once for all the landlord class, which played the triple role of landlord, tax-collector, and usurer, as the deadly obstacle to strong central government.

Having put the land-reform program into effect, the new regime applied a parallel process to businessmen in urban centers. The "Five-anti Movement" of 1952 was theoretically a drive to punish those guilty of bribery, tax evasion, stealing state property, theft of state economic secrets, and embezzlement in carrying out government contracts. In actuality, this was a campaign intended to cripple the money power of the merchants and manufacturers and cow them into submission to the new order. The movement lasted only a few months, but it speedily liquidated the firms on the government's black list as "lawbreakers" under one or the other of the five crimes.

Even more terrorizing was the campaign against "counterrevolutionaries" in 1951, during which scores of thousands were put to death as enemies of the state, while many others were sentenced to forced labor. This campaign was intended to instill fear of the authority of Peking in the people as a whole. It was a calculated move to demonstrate the power of the new government, to give the public a sampling of the iron hand it could employ. It was a sort of *"hsia ma wai"* ("warrior's prowess upon hopping off his horse") or shock treatment on the arrival of the new conqueror. Unlike other reigns of terror in history, this movement did not get out of control. As soon as the intended purpose was achieved, Peking wound up the drive.

Finally, in October 1953, Peking ordered a reorganization of the regional governments in pursuit of a policy for greater centralization of authority. Since 1949 the country had been divided into six Administrative Regions, which formed an intermediate level between the central government and the provincial governments and were ruled by Military and Administrative Committees. The new order replaced the latter with Administrative Committees having greatly reduced powers. In the following year the Administrative Regions were abolished altogether, the central government assuming direct control over the provinces. The object of these moves was to forestall the rise of the age-old tendencies toward regionalism, which could seriously obstruct the central government in the gigantic tasks ahead. The subsequent defeat of Kao Kang and his plot to set up "independent kingdoms" bore proof of the importance of this policy. That Peking was successful is evident from the absence of repercussions in support of Kao and his cohorts.

All these measures were of vital importance to reconstruction because they greatly strengthened the stability of the regime. To conserve and increase production, to widen the power of state control, and to liquidate potential opposition were the three dimensions of Communist recovery in the years 1949–53. In China's past history the power of a new regime was often broken by one or more of these disruptive influences: economic dislocation and collapse; corruption of government and military personnel; passive resistance of landlords and city merchants; regional insubordination and its centrifugal consequences. As a result of the measures taken by Peking in the first four years of its rule, none of these trends occurred. It may be recalled that these were the years when China was deeply involved in the Korean conflict, which imposed a serious strain on her economy. Yet Peking managed to move ahead with its plans for industrial construction. The soundness of the country's economic structure was largely attributable to the influence of the measures indicated above. By the middle of 1953, the essential conditions had been created for embarking on the main tasks of reconstruction.

The central program of reconstruction revolves around the dual tasks of industralization and socialization of agriculture. These two tasks, interrelated but each stupendous in itself, are engaging the primary attention of the Communist state builders. Upon their success or failure depends the fate of the regime in Peking and with it the destiny of the Chinese people. One must not let the so-called cold war between China and the Western powers overshadow these vital trends of development going on inside China. The cold war is one of the consequences of the resurgence of the Chinese nation; but the industrial and agricultural programs being carried out inside China constitute the basis of that resurgence itself. The real history of the new China is being made in the tens of thousands of villages in ferment and in the new factories and railroads emerging throughout the country rather than over short-wave broadcasts or international conference tables.

Let us begin with the socialization of agriculture. We have seen how land reform was first launched at the inception of the Communist movement in Kiangsi, how it was extended to North China during the war years, and how the law of 1950 ordered the reform on a nationwide scale. The year 1952 when the Land Reform Law of 1950 became a reality throughout the country may be considered the culmination of the era of land reform. The purpose of the entire movement was to eliminate the landlord class; its background was the exploitation of mass discontent for the seizure of power; and its method was the equalization of landholdings. This is, however, already a thing of the past. Immediately upon the completion of land reform, Communist policy moved forward to what is called the "transition to socialism." By socialization of agriculture, the Communists mean that their policy is not to stop at land reform, but is to march forward to the ultimate goal of socialism in agriculture by means of collectivization. In other words, the view entertained during the war years by many observers that the Chinese Communists were advocates of agrarian reform as an end in itself is fundamentally erroneous. Investing the masses with ownership of redistributed land, which brought the Communists to power, was only a means to an end, not an end in itself. The peasantry was aroused by land reform and other measures, not because the Communists wanted to create a country of landowning farmers, but because they wanted to use this to build up their own power.

The real objective of the Communists today is quite

contrary in spirit to the land-reform movement. Only yesterday the Communists were redistributing the land to the peasants; but today they are replacing redistribution with group farming. Only yesterday their slogan was equalization of holdings; but today they are seeking to obliterate the concept of private ownership of land. Only yesterday their consuming passion was to eliminate the landlords; but today they are making the state the sole owner of the land and seeking to turn all the peasants into laborers for the state. Land reform, which subverted the old society, is itself being subverted today by the counter-movement of socialization. It is of the utmost importance for us to keep this change of policy clearly in mind; for in any given area the new process of socialization follows so closely upon the heels of the old process of land reform, and the two merge into each other so subtly, that the actual metamorphosis is apt to become a reality before its import even occurs to those most directly affected.

The logic underlying such a radical shift of policy is not far to seek. Land reform is an indispensable step, because without it the landlord class could not have been overthrown and all subsequent measures could not have been undertaken. This is the reason why the Communists have consistently maintained through the years that the Chinese Revolution must pass through a bourgeois-democratic stage before it can reach the ultimate stage of socialism. The bourgeois-democratic stage has also been known as their minimum program (or present program), while the socialist stage is called the maximum program (or future program). The minimum program denotes a bourgeois-democratic revolution led by the joint dictatorship of several revolutionary classes to overthrow the landlord and

other classes of reaction, while the maximum program denotes the ultimate socialist revolution led by the proletariat. The present transition is from the bourgeois-democratic revolution to the socialist revolution. Without
the successful fulfillment of the minimum program, the
achievement of the maximum program is out of the question. Hence the haste in completing the land-reform movement.

But with the overthrow of the landlords, the usefulness
to the Communists of the system of land redistribution or
equalization has ceased. In other words, the Communists
have no use for the minimum program *per se;* it is significant to them only as a prelude to the maximum program.
Thus it is that the progression from land reform to socialization (or collectivization) must be immediate and continuous. The Communists cannot possibly tolerate the rise
of a new landowning class. Since land is virtually the only
source of wealth in China, to leave it in the hands of the
people, as is done under the land-reform program, and thus
court the formation of a new class of landowners, is a potential threat to the Communist regime. This explains the
current drive to socialize agriculture. The Communists
have been perfectly consistent with regard to the time
sequence of these stages. Only outside observers have allowed themselves to imagine that the Communists would
content themselves with the minimum and would not go
forward with the maximum program.

In any event, it is beyond doubt that the Communists
are firmly determined to carry out the maximum program.
Admittedly, the Communists recognize that the task of
socialization of agriculture is not to be accomplished in
a few years. It has to take time, and can be carried out only

by progressive stages. But one stage must lead to another of more intensified socialization until collectivization is finally achieved. This accounts for the new organizational measures now being enforced in the country. As they are steps looking toward ultimate collectivization, they can best be called measures of semi-collectivization.

The first and most elementary of these measures of semi-collectivization is the formation of the mutual-aid teams. The mutual-aid team is a system of group farming under which the member peasants help one another with their labor at the time of planting, cultivating, and harvesting. This is the short-term type of mutual-aid team, for group activity is limited to the pooling of labor during the busy season. It is the very first step in co-operative agriculture, which the Communist government attempts to introduce in a given area immediately upon the completion of land redistribution. In the Yenan days the labor-exchange brigades bore many characteristics of the mutual-aid teams of today. On the basis of tested success in the case of the labor-exchange brigades, the Communists have been pushing the formation of the mutual-aid teams over the entire country. Inasmuch as Chinese villages have been accustomed to such mutual help through the ages, this type of mutual-aid team is easily set up. But there is this basic difference: mutual aid was voluntary and sporadic in pre-Communist days; it is now systematically led and enforced by party cadres. Formerly co-operation was laissez-faire and innocuous; but today the process is driven by a political motivation—namely, to move on through successive stages to full collectivization.

The next stage of stronger group farming is the long-term type of mutual-aid team. Here the peasant members of the team not only help one another with labor, but also pool their draft animals (such as the water buffalo) and farm equipment. Moreover, this co-operation is not limited to one particular season. The team is set up to last from one season to another without being broken up until, at an appropriate date, it is merged into the next stage of more intensified co-operation. As a rule, the short-term type does not exist for more than two or three years in a given area before the party cadres lead the peasant members into the long-term type. At this point they are prepared to pause a little, in order to develop a complete acceptance by the peasants before moving into the next stage.

In both the short-term and the long-term type of mutual-aid team, effective ownership of his own land is exercised by the individual peasant. Each peasant selects the crop he wishes to plant on his land. When the crop is harvested, he keeps the crop, though the sale of whatever surplus he may have as well as the purchase of his necessities are handled through government-controlled co-operative agencies. Varying with different localities, the peasants pay from 18 to 27 per cent of their crop to the government as tax, in addition to certain special contributions and levies. Under this situation the lot of the majority of the rural population (that is, the poor peasants and the landless peasants of pre-Communist days) is considerably improved. Even allowing for the highest tax rate and for the special contributions to the government, they still can keep well over 50 per cent of their produce. This is perhaps the main reason why the Communist government has kept the support of the masses and why it has been successful in moving so rapidly from one form of group farming to another.

The third stage in co-operative agriculture is marked by the formation of the producers' co-operatives. A producers' co-operative usually embraces a number of mutual-aid teams. It is therefore much larger in size. The distinguishing feature here, however, is the pooling of land, in addition to the pooling of labor, draft animals, and farm equipment. For while private ownership of land is still respected in principle, yet in actuality the land of the different members of the co-operative is cultivated on a collective basis. No individual decision is permitted in the choice of the crops to be planted. The cadres in control of the co-operative decide in joint consultation with the members. Then, when the crop is harvested, a certain prior portion is set aside as government tax. The next portion is earmarked for the purchase of seed for the following planting season. The balance is divided among the members on the basis of what each of them has invested in accordance with the following ratio: land, 30 per cent; labor, 60 per cent; and equipment, 10 per cent. As can readily be seen, the spirit of socialization is much more pronounced in the producers' co-operative than in the mutual-aid team. These co-operatives are collectives in fact though not in name. Yet the Communists are moving ahead, for so long as the livelihood of the peasants is better than it was in pre-Communist days, they can be made to go along with the system.

The producers' co-operatives represent the limit of the Communist effort at socializing agriculture to date. It is reported that approximately 65 per cent of China's total farm households were organized into mutual-aid teams by the spring of 1955, and approximately 12 per cent into producers' co-operatives. (The next step will be the creation of collective farms. This system has just barely made its beginnings in Manchuria. The government is using these initial experiments to demonstrate the advantages of collectivization to the peasants. It may require another five years for these farms to assume any substantial importance.) The trend of progression from one type to another, however, is as irresistible as the drive from the top is unrelenting. It is true that participation by the peasants in these types is voluntary. But as membership means correct political status and carries with it prior access to credit, seeds, farm loans, and equipment, it is doubtful whether there is any peasant who can afford to remain out of this system sponsored by the government.

The stupendous nature of these measures is self-evident. What is at stake involves 80 per cent of the nation's population of 580,000,000. The proposed plan means no less than repudiating the policy of land redistribution and demanding of this vast mass of humanity that it submit to a new socialist state in which the real owner of the land is the government while the present farmers will become no more than regimented teams of laborers working for the government. In this connection, a great variety of opinion has been expressed by experts outside of China on its problems, hazards, and possible outcome. One school of thought directs major attention to the dim outlook for increased production. It holds that neither under the fragmentation of landholdings following land redistribution nor under the collective farming of the producers' cooperatives will Communist China be able to increase her agricultural production substantially. The reasons given are her lack of the capital resources necessary to reclaim large areas of land and to introduce mechanization, modern implements, and high-potency fertilizers. And so long as she cannot step up her production, they conclude that Communist China cannot win with her socialization program. Another school is concerned over the bulging population of China. The existing population is 580,000,000. But the yearly increase is about 8,000,000. Despite Communist denunciation of the Malthusian theory, these experts can look forward to nothing except growing unemployment and further lowering of the standard of living. Experts of still another school see in the creeping rate of advance represented by the mutual-aid teams and producers' co-operatives a basic fear of peasant resistance. In their opinion, the Chinese peasants are die-hard individualists who will rise in bitter opposition to Peking's attempt to take land away from them. The Communist leaders, according to these observers, are treading on a suicidal path in trying to impose collectivization on the Chinese peasant, to whom the good earth means his very life. The leaders, so successful in equalizing land for the benefit of the peasants, are simply playing with fire in taking land away from them. These observers further point out that unlike Soviet Russia, Peking is not in a position to use the same ruthless methods that were employed by Russia in its struggle to compel the farmers to submit to collectivization. The peasants form the sole backbone of the Chinese Communist power, while Russian Communism could rely on an industrial proletariat to offset the farmers.

Do these observations touch the core of Communist planning? Can these opinions, obviously pertinent as far as they go, have escaped the attention of the Communist leaders, or have they failed to receive primary attention because there are greater issues at stake? It is important to remember that in the eyes of the Red leaders such questions as increase in production, unemployment, the ratio of population to food and possible peasant reaction are all relatively secondary in importance. Their principal concern is that the socialization of agriculture be carried out, because there is no alternative for them if they want to perpetuate their regime. This paramount need overshadows every other consideration. The Communists, who have risen to power on peasant strength, certainly know better than anyone else how terrifying peasant strength can be. Having utilized that power to overthrow the Kuomintang, they dare not leave the way open for others to follow in their own footsteps and wrest power from them. To prevent such a process of retribution, they feel constrained to close the fountain of strength in the peasantry once for all. This is the fundamental reason underlying the Communist haste to implement a program of collectivization.

In Communist planning, the nationalization of land has now become a *sine qua non* for the perpetuation of power. So long as land is privately owned, and so long as the exchange of landownership is permitted between individuals, the government always faces the danger of losing its tight control. For under private ownership a new landlordism, based upon new concentrations of landownership, is bound to arise. Such a development would bring about two consequences, both detrimental to any existing government. First, a new independent class of wealth could through its economic power dictate terms to the government. Second, the growing disparity between the rich and the poor would tend inevitably to accumulate economic and social discontent, the solution of which would in time become increasingly difficult for the govern-

ment. The mutual-aid teams and producers' co-operatives
are steps clearly designed to obliterate the trend toward
private ownership and to forestall private land transactions. Thus any concentration of land in the hands of a
new social class of influence seems out of the question.

From the standpoint of historical experience, the Communists are further convinced that if they had stopped with
land redistribution, they would have made a serious mistake. Land-reform measures, as noted previously, are not
new in China. Numerous instances can be found in past
history. Such reforms sought to set a ceiling on maximum
individual holdings, and to distribute surplus holdings or
the abandoned lands to poor peasants. But big landlords
inevitably arose, and private land transactions continued
without interruption. The Communists are determined
not to let history repeat itself. First, their land redistribution of 1950 was so thorough that the landlords as a class
were wiped out. Second, after land redistribution, they
immediately followed with "transition to socialism." By
this they aim to make the state the sole landlord and to
make the entire agricultural population a vast mass of
farmer workers for the state. Apparently the Communists
consider that the sooner collectivization is pushed forward,
the easier their task will be. Peasant resistance is less likely
to develop at the present time, because the great majority
of peasants were never used to owning land. But it might
develop if the people were allowed to enjoy the sense of
private landownership for a longer period of time. Collectivization would be difficult in that event. Hence the immediate enforcement of the "transition to socialism."

No doubt the Communists have also drawn lessons from
Russia. After observing her experience, they are all the

more convinced that the land must be nationalized as soon as is feasible. Lenin's policy of giving the land back to peasants proved detrimental to the government. As a result, Stalin pushed collectivization at all costs. Stalin's thesis that the socialization of industry cannot be successfully carried out without the socialization of agriculture certainly has had a decisive influence on the policy of Peking. It may safely be said that the Chinese Communists' determination to socialize agriculture after the 1950 land redistribution is patterned upon the Soviet experience in the post-Lenin era.

In answer to her critics, Peking seems to have a special set of reasons that justify her policy and her confidence that she can succeed with the program of collectivization. The Communists seem to think that, low as China's agricultural production is, the greatest evil in the past was the poor distribution of the available output. One of the outstanding objectives of Communist policy today is to centralize grain-collection in the hands of the government and to enable the government to divert a prior portion of the country's agricultural output to the urgent needs of the state, such as the industrialization and maintenance of its huge civil and military establishments. The control that Peking exercises through the mutual-aid teams and producers' co-operatives meets this objective very well. Even the peasants who have not yet been organized into these groups are participating in the supply and marketing co-operatives, through which alone they can sell their products to government trading companies and procure their daily necessities. Obviously Peking regards the distribution and control of the available agricultural output as far more important than its increase. This does not mean that

Peking does not desire to stimulate production; but if the increase of production were to require an investment of capital beyond the means of the government, then the immediate stress would be placed on a state grain-collection program. Nor is the government in favor of a free grain market. For while it offers certain incentives to farmers to intensify cultivation, the government can still lose control of the movement of grain. Hence along with the state grain-collection program, Peking further stresses the policy of a state-controlled grain market.

It is the central thesis of the Communist leaders that such measures of semi-collectivization as they have put into effect need not bring unbearable hardship to the peasants, in spite of the statistics of foreign economic experts. To be sure, Peking wants to take a great share of the total agricultural output for the use of the state. To be sure, until the state's quota is met, the peasantry will bear the brunt of the much publicized "austerity" and "bitter struggle" which lie ahead. To be sure, Peking does not have the capital to introduce fertilizers or improved farm equipment which might otherwise increase farm productivity. But it can point to the following factors that would operate in favor of the new program. First, the government will take from the peasants no more than the margin that used to go to the landlords. This is a point of fundamental importance in considering the distribution of China's wealth today. As has been shown above, the taxes paid by the peasants, even including special levies, are still less than the portion they were required to surrender to the landlords. Thus even if the country's agricultural output registers only a fractional increase or no increase at all, the situation cannot become explosive. Second, as taxes collected no longer go through the medium of the landlord class, there is no longer abuse in this direction. Whatever is paid by the peasants does reach the government. This works well both for the taxpayer and for the government. Third, as for the middle peasants, they will live with no more but also no less than formerly. Fourth, the poor and landless peasants of the old days will live considerably better than before. With these paupers of a bygone age the sense of property is extremely weak. The tradition of being hired as a retainer in exchange for a bowl of rice is more familiar. So long as the bowl of rice is forthcoming under the care of the state, the measures for collectivization are a matter of relatively little concern to them. It cannot be denied that the majority of the poor Chinese peasants are more interested in having food to eat than in owning land for its own sake.

Furthermore, the new government is carrying on important projects, involving extensive use of manpower but little capital outlay, for water conservancy, irrigation, and reclamation of waste and semi-waste land. By these measures it expects to have new acreage for production. Peking frankly proposes to put the masses to work, and expects such extensive use of manpower both to increase productivity and to absorb the population bulge. As Chou En-lai has said: "We have a vast area and much uncultivated land. Our river-valley and irrigation projects will need much labor. A population problem therefore does not exist." Chou may be too sweeping in his generalizations. It is clear, however, that Peking looks at the problem differently from the way Western economists assess it. Western economists maintain that China's rate of industrial growth cannot increase fast enough to defeat the Malthusian theory. Indeed, it would be impossible to defeat the Malthusian theory, and some sort of population problem will exist. But there is also much practicability and common sense in what Chou says. Peking does not have the capital to purchase large quantities of farm fertilizer or farm equipment. As a result, the government will intensify the use of labor to make up for the lack of capital. The surplus population, or a great part of it, can maintain itself by being absorbed in this process of stimulating production through the greatly expanded use of labor.

Among other factors in Peking's favor, one must also count the work of the party cadres, teaching the peasants more scientific methods of farming. This is another inexpensive way of stimulating output. Through the mutual-aid teams the farmers are taught how to prevent crop damage, the methods of pruning trees and selecting better seed, a more effective use of grain stalks for fertilizing, and the importance of a timetable for drying the grain and plowing the fields. Last but not least, peace and stability have made such a radical change in the people's lives that there is a better and fuller utilization of land and a happier distribution of whatever is produced on it.

By setting these factors against the hazards, the Communists believe that the balance will be in their favor. Their determination to move on toward the socialization of agriculture is therefore unquestioned. The only qualifying factors concern the time it will take and the extent to which the program is to be carried at various stages of the process. It is significant that the announced target of creating 800,000 producers' co-operatives by the end of 1957 will absorb only 20 per cent of the rural households. It is altogether possible that the period of such interim measures as the mutual-aid teams and producers' co-operatives will be drawn out over a considerable time. Such a procedure would be characteristic of the flexibility of the Communist leaders of China. They may be expected to push their program for socialization of agriculture as far as they can safely go, and halt wherever it is necessary.

The Communist approach is one of *"kan chou chien shih"* ("combined application of stiffness and softness"). In the gigantic bid for socialization, the authorities in Peking caution against both passivity and precipitate action. The cadres are admonished not to use coercion, for fear of arousing resistance in the peasants, but at the same time they are to set up additional teams and co-operatives according to schedule. Under a policy of seeming moderation and caution, there is positiveness of will and drive. A temporary drop in production or the slackening of collective effort in a given locality does not seem to alarm the Communist government. Its leaders plead patience, for collectivization needs time to take effect. But in reality there is an unrelenting vigilance over the nation's total grain output, a feverish race to expand the mutual-aid teams and producers' co-operatives, and an absolute prohibition of any recurrence of landlordism. This is admittedly a period of "transition to socialism." Mao and his associates are quite content to give the people the psychological satisfaction to be derived from private ownership of land, thus avoiding the danger of peasant resistance, while they themselves reap the actual benefit of the collectives without arousing the peasants' fears of collectivization. In fact, the peasant proprietors are today producing in much the same way as they would on a large collective farm. If this is how Mao "scientifically and systematically" applies Marxism-Leninism to the "concrete problems of the Chinese Revolution," it must be said that the solution is clever and practicable.

The only remaining question is: when will full collectivization come about? No doubt Peking will stretch as far as she can afford her present policy of patient and gradual advance in an effort to lead peacefully to the goal of socialism. But it is entirely possible that such a policy will bring only a partial success—for example, success in certain areas but not in others. In such an event, Peking will be constrained to rely upon new strength derived from sources other than the agricultural program, and to employ this new strength to compel all areas to accept full collectivization. Perhaps full collectivization will have to wait till the industrialization program has progressed to a point where the regime is so entrenched in its industrial and military power that it is no longer afraid to dictate its terms to the peasantry. When that day comes, Chinese Communism, like its counterpart in Russia, will not hesitate to use forcible measures to complete collectivization. We must therefore turn our attention to Peking's second great task, its program for industrialization.

Parelleling the effort to socialize agriculture, Peking's industrialization program is likewise characterized by boldness and a determination to win. Reference has already been made to the rapid industrial recovery in the years immediately following 1949. During this recovery the policy of the new government was not one of laissez-faire, but one of progressive nationalization. The so-called state sector of China's economy steadily extended its scope and closed the ring on the private-capitalist sector. With itself constituted as a virtual supertrust and manipulating all instruments of control in the fields of banking and trade as well as industry, Peking faced little difficulty in squeezing out private industry and business and placing most of the nation's industries under state control. By the end of 1954 almost all of the existing heavy industry and well over sixty per cent of the light industry had been nationalized. Whatever was left out of the state sector was in effect also under strict government control, inasmuch as the government enjoyed the sole power of allocating raw materials, bank loans, and means of transportation.

In the midst of this drive for nationalization, the launching of the ambitious Five-Year Plan was announced by Peking in mid-1953, following lengthy negotiations with Russia. Peking had worked out her preliminary blueprint of the plan before negotiations were initiated with Russia in August 1952; but as she was dependent on Russian assistance, the final version of the plan was not completed until mid-1953. The basic spirit of the Five-Year Plan is that China seeks to emulate the example of Soviet Russia —that is, to begin with the creation of heavy industry, and achieve success in record time. In the thinking of the Communist planners, China does not have the time to spend in moving slowly from light industry to heavy and defense industries over a period of half a century or a century, as did the Western nations. China's salvation, according to them, lies in the speedy establishment of heavy and defense industries so that she will be strong and independent within a matter of one or two decades. In order to achieve this, the people are told that they must be prepared for a shortage of consumer goods. But in exchange for such sacrifices and "bitter struggle," they will have guns and tanks, factories and power plants, trucks and mechanized equipment, all of which provide the sinews of a modern world power. As Chou En-lai said poignantly at a recent People's Congress, "to bear certain hardships and inconveniences in order that in the long run we shall live in prosperity and happiness" is infinitely better than "to seek petty benefits now and thus never be able to shake off poverty and backwardness."

Specifically, the program calls for the construction and renovation of over 600 industrial projects during the period of the plan, from 1953 to 1957. These projects cover a wide variety of industries, notably mining, iron and steel, electric power, oil refining, metalworks, chemicals, and railroads. Of the total of 600 projects, 141 outstanding units are to be constructed with Soviet equipment and help, in accordance with an economic agreement concluded in September 1953. In 1954, 15 more units were added, making a total of 156 enterprises under Soviet sponsorship. These projects are to be completed within a seven-year period commencing with 1953. According to the terms of the agreement, China will pay for the Soviet equipment and help with grain and other raw materials. It is obvious that in scale and importance these projects top the list of the entire program.

The location and distribution of the major centers of the new industries are interesting. Manchuria remains one of the key areas. Thus Anshan is one of the great steel centers; there new furnaces and mills are being added to those already in operation. At Fushun, new mechanized mines of coal are being built. However, a new iron and steel center is being created at Paotou, in Suiyuan, the hub of the old caravan trade leading into Turkistan and Central Asia. This will draw upon the iron deposits of Pailingmiao and the coal of Tatung. This new complex in the northwest portends the conversion of that area into a giant industrial belt. A third center of the iron and coal industries lies in the mid-Yangtze valley. But Tayeh with its iron and steel mills, and Pinghsiang with its coal, represent more or less an expansion of what already existed there.

There is no doubt that under the Five-Year Plan the country's principal energies are to be concentrated in the northeast and northwest. Electric power plants are being developed in more scattered cities: Chengchow, Taiyuan, Sian, Tihwa (Urumchi), and Chungking. Yumen (in Kansu) and Yenchang (in Shensi) are to be centers of the petroleum industry, while new rich oil deposits have been prospected farther west in the Tarim and Dzungaria basins on both sides of the Tienshan range. In this latter area it is also reported that rich deposits of uranium have spurred new researches into the development of atomic weapons. Most ambitious of all is the construction of three major railroads: (1) the Paotou-Lanchow line; (2) the Lanchow-Tihwa line, extending westward to Alma Ata in Soviet territory; and (3) Tienshui-Chengtu-Kweiyang-Kunming line. As for machine production, Taiyuan is emerging as the leading center; there a mammoth, up-to-date plant will be the first to turn out steel-rolling equipment and heavy engineering products. Peking and Tientsin are the locale for metal-working industries. Perhaps the least emphasis is placed by Communist planning on the Shanghai area, which used to be the center of China's industries. Here the existing textile mills and small machine works will continue to operate, but clearly the Five-Year Plan seeks to shift the center of gravity away from the seaboard region to the great north and northwest.

In discussing the progress of the Five-Year Plan, it is important to bear in mind that the enterprises mentioned above are in the initial construction stage, with all its attendant difficulties and impediments. For this reason, actual accomplishments are often below target figures. Thus of the total construction planned for the five-year period, the year 1953 achieved no more than 12 per cent, and 1954 no more than another 15 per cent, leaving 73 per cent for the three years remaining. It is quite possible that by 1957 the target figures will not be realized fully. But a certain lag in meeting the targets need not be construed as a sign of the failure of the Five-Year Plan. It is more important to recognize that the major portion of the plan is actually being carried out.

In any event, it is as important to see what the Communist government expects to achieve in point of aggregate industrial output by 1957 as it is to note the slow rate of progress in the initial years. According to Communist estimates released in the summer of 1955, the crude-steel output in 1957 is expected to be three times that of 1952 (or over 4.1 million metric tons); the coal output in 1957 about two times that of 1952 (or 113 million metric tons); the electric power generating capacity in 1957 over two times that of 1952 (or 16 billion killowatt-hours); and the oil output in 1957 seven times that of 1952 (or 1.5 million metric tons).

These figures, when set alongside the current industrial production of the United States or of the Soviet Union, are of course very small indeed. But such a comparison is almost meaningless. Even when compared with the record of modern Japan or with the results of the first Soviet Five-Year Plan, it is extremely doubtful whether by 1957 China's heavy industries will have reached a level equal to that achieved by Russia in 1932 or by Japan in the 1930's. Experts believe that China's industrial strength at the completion of the Five-Year Plan can outrank the strength only of such countries as Canada, Belgium, and India.

The effectiveness of the Plan must not, however, be judged by contemporary Western standards. Rather it should be viewed against the Chinese. background. Crude-steel production, with a prewar peak of 900,000 metric tons and a 1949 level of 150,000 metric tons, is to be raised to 4,100,000 in 1957. Coal production with a prewar peak of 59,000,000 metric tons and a 1949 level of 26,000,000 metric tons, is to be raised to 113,000,000. The electric power generating capacity was 6 billion kw-h in the peak year before the war, dropped to 3.6 billion kw-h in 1949, but will be increased to 16 billion kw-h by 1957. The crude-oil production, which amounted to only 330,000 metric tons in the prewar peak year and 125,000 in 1949, will hit the high-water mark of 1,500,000 metric tons. For China to attain the growth outlined in these figures represents tremendous progress by her own standards. It is the differential between the old and new stages in her own industrial life rather than the absolute figure that should furnish the yardstick by which to measure the increase in her strength.

China has huge manpower. No doubt Peking will use it to offset her weakness in capital resources to a considerable degree. The great experience of the building of the Burma Road and of the airfields during World War II has demonstrated how the Chinese people, under proper organization and direction, can accomplish maximum results with minimum material resources. Under the Communist regime this trend has been further intensified. In the Hwai

River valley project, for example, mass utilization of human labor has built dams which bear eloquent testimony to the greatness of the nation. In the middle stream of the river, eight lakes with a storage capacity of 7.5 billion cubic yards of water, plus dikes along their perimeters, were built by hand labor in two years. At times as many as two million workers toiled on the project, digging earth and building culverts, sluices, and dikes.

Furthermore, Peking is pushing the process of industrialization in a desperate race for time. The amount of capital available, both from China's own resources and from the meager Soviet aid, is indeed limited. But whatever it has at its command is put to quick and effective use. Once the foundation is built, the increase in growth will be expedited. Such an efficient utilization of limited resources can go a long way to balance certain shortages of capital goods. In this connection, the Ten-Year Plan outlined by General Chiang Kai-shek in his *China's Destiny* (1943) is of interest. Of course, this plan never had a chance of execution. But at the time, it was frankly admitted in Chungking that the program could not be carried through without large-scale foreign capital. The Minister of Economic Affairs at that time spoke in terms of importing ten billion dollars' worth of capital goods shortly after the war. The distinguishing feature of the Communist industrialization program today is the ability of Peking to work with a direct and practicable plan, within the framework of China's own resources and the very limited Soviet aid, which in ten years will not aggregate more than one billion dollars. The surprising aspect thus is not how little is being accomplished but that, however little, a substantial beginning is being made. As far as internal reconstruction is concerned, the Chinese Communists certainly bear the mark of the go-getter. Rather than wait for ten billion, they work with the few hundred million that are immediately obtainable. Their philosophy is to accomplish a positive start right away. If less than one billion can make the targets mentioned above, then immeasurably greater programs can be undertaken whenever the ten-billion large-scale foreign aid is made available.

While the world is absorbed in the cold war, the energies of 580,000,000 people are being turned to the completion of the basic industries under a compelling sense of urgency. Not a day or a week is wasted. The next ten years will bring forth the nucleus of a new industrial state. It will be smaller, to be sure, than the American or Soviet giant, but it will be powerful by the standards of continental Asia. In this respect the highest traditions of industriousness and ingenuity of the Chinese people as well as of modern technology will leave their indelible marks on the epic of the new China.

This policy of quick industrialization within limited means is not without its drawbacks. The immediate concentration is clearly on short-term gains, leaving long-term growth to the future. Heavy and defense industries are receiving an overwhelming priority, almost to the neglect of light and consumer industries. In the rush for time, installations and technical personnel fall short of the desired level. Moreover, China cannot attain full industrial growth without access to large volumes of foreign capital. At a certain point in the future, she will find the one-sided slant of her economy grievously inadequate for her needs. Likewise, she will find that there is a limit beyond which she cannot dig further into her own available resources. But

the important point to bear in mind is that Peking's calculation at present seems to stress the need of building a
nucleus, a quick start in her industrialization. This nucleus
China aims to set up in the shortest possible time, in order
to furnish the minimum requirements of her large armed
forces. After that base has been won, she will re-think her
plans. Perhaps it is Peking's view that with such a strong
base, she will be better able to explore new sources of capital for greater development.

The significant point in the entire industrialization program is the fact that the center of gravity lies in the Manchuria, Suiyuan-Kansu, and Sinkiang broad belt. The pres-
ence of natural resources and the proximity to Russia no
doubt are important factors in the selection of this great
northern region. Nevertheless, other considerations of
high-level state planning seem to have played an equally
decisive role. There is clearly a determination to withdraw
from the southeastern seaboard. Meantime, while the existing industrial base in Manchuria is being utilized for
speedy expansion, Peking is seeking to avoid an undue concentration in that area. Instead, the Communist plan is to
extend the new industrial belt westward through Chahar,
Suiyuan, and Kansu into Sinkiang. The significance of this
type of planning is indeed far-reaching. For one thing, to
build China's industrial and military base in this region,
which in past ages was a power vacuum used by the
Hsiung-nu, Khitan, Hsien-pi, Tu-chüeh, and Mongols as
their stamping-grounds, is sound strategy from the standpoint of national defense as a whole. Then, too, the policy
of dispersion through the different sections of the entire
northern belt will obviate any dependence on a massive
industrial build-up in Manchuria. The danger of a possi-

ble "independent kingdom" arising in Manchuria must have prompted the Communist planners to develop the steel center at Paotou and to launch the three major trunk railroads for Kansu, Sinkiang, Szechuan, and the other western provinces.

But overshadowing all other considerations in importance is the effect of the northern industrial belt on the future division of China into an industrial north and an agricultural south, which in turn will have a direct bearing on the perpetuation of the power of the Communist regime. Population in the northern belt is not so dense as in Central and South China. Here the extension of the co-operatives is possible without any great dislocation of the rural economy. The collectivization of agriculture can be carried out more quickly and more successfully in the north than in the other areas. On the other hand, Central and South China are heavily populated and embrace the regions of most intensive farming. It cannot be assumed with any degree of certainty that full collectivization will not cause disaffection. The hope for the ultimate socialist state, then, should logically be based in the north. In all likelihood, the paramount consideration in the minds of the Communist leaders is the fact that, should trouble develop in Central and South China, an unassailable fortress in the north will always command a decisive advantage in suppressing rebellion or opposition. With Peking committed to the socialization of agriculture on a nationwide scale, this becomes a particularly relevant precaution on the part of the Communist planners. The day may well come when the Communist regime finds it necessary to mobilize the industrial strength of the north to cope with the opposition of the agricultural south. In such an event a great northern industrial empire will almost indisputably hold the key to victory.

The Five-Year Plan, then, by creating an industrial north and an agricultural south, may well revolutionize China's history once again from the standpoint of the relative importance of her geographical sections. From antiquity till the An-shih Revolt (755–763), the north commanded decisive superiority. The north with Chang-an and Shensi as the center of gravity was then self-sufficient and not dependent upon the south. During the Sung dynasty, however, the self-sufficiency of the north broke down. The establishment of the Sung capital at Kaifeng (in Honan) put an end to the political pre-eminence of Chang-an and Shensi, while the southward movement of Chinese power under the pressure of the Juchens put the south on a par with the north as a center of political leadership. When the Mongols established their capital in Peking, the reassertion of the north as a base for political and military leadership was seriously compromised by its economic dependence on the south. With no industrialization or other measures for economic independence, the north throughout the Ming and Ch'ing dynasties and under the Republic had to reckon with the wealth of the south. While wars and invasions followed one another in the north, the south was almost consistently marked by stability, rich agriculture, and cultural development. Thus the south enjoyed a great leverage in national affairs. In the early part of this century, considerable industrialization took place in Manchuria. But it was largely the work of the Japanese and benefited only the local warlords.

Now the industrialization program of the Communists promises to revolutionize the situation for the first time in about five hundred years. The Five-Year Plan is destined to build up the north and once again make it the overlord of the south. The resultant situation will be somewhat similar to that which existed prior to the end of the T'ang. North China will regain its supremacy, economically as well as politically and militarily. The great northwest will again become the center of gravity, as Shensi was in the old days. The difference is that while pre-T'ang China looked upon the Yangtze as virtually its southern frontier, the new industrial north will seek to use its superior strength to demand undisputed control over the rich agricultural areas of all of Central and South China. The importance of the Five-Year Plan indeed cannot be overstated.

Viewed in this way, there exists an intimate interrelationship between Peking's dual tasks of industrialization and socialization of agriculture. We have said above that Peking is moving with caution and flexibility in its bid for collectivization. Interim measures for semi-collectivization may well be carried on for a considerable time. Peking is stressing the co-operative aspects of the current measures, hoping that they will win increased popular support as it becomes possible to provide better equipment and show better results. Certainly Peking will hesitate to enforce full collectivization before she builds up a powerful industrial base sufficient to enable her to crush possible peasant opposition. Once that industrial base is achieved, however, Peking need not hesitate to push its agricultural policy to its logical conclusion. When that day arrives, should popular support not be forthcoming in Central and South China, Peking may well resort to repressive and ruthless measures against the recalcitrant peasantry. It is indeed a grim prospect, but it is not improbable. The challenge of the Five-Year Plan thus overshadows everything else. If Peking makes this hurdle, her claim to long-term control of China will largely be won. Hence the great urgency attached to the Five-Year Plan. Hence also the selection of the great northern belt as the seat for the new industries.

The over-all Communist state planning then is fairly clear. The first order of business is to continue the interim measures of semi-collectivization of agriculture and at the same time to push the minimum basis of industrialization (such as is envisaged in the Five-Year Plan) to a speedy success. The next stage will be full collectivization. When that day comes, the Communists will be strongly entrenched in the industrial north, against which it will be almost useless for the agricultural south to revolt. With diligence, patience, and perseverance, the Communists believe that they can overcome the difficulties and achieve their goal. All other considerations along the road to this grand climax appear to be only secondary in importance.

So far the Communist leadership of both revolution and reconstruction within the borders of China has been an uninterrupted success. To be sure, China has a long way to go yet in her tasks of reconstruction. But a sound beginning is taking shape, and the leaders in Peking are confident. If they can achieve the same success with the great problems ahead as they did in solving their past problems, the attainment of an internal strength commensurate with China's new position in Asia can be expected. More than any other factor involved in the current world tension or ideological conflict, this will form the permanent force in the emergence of a new order in the Far East.

VI

THE OUTLOOK: PEACE OR WAR?

❁

As we look into the future, no one can deny the fact that Communist China has emerged as a great continental power in Asia. Internally, in spite of the totalitarian rule of the Communist elite, she has achieved peace and unification. The effectiveness of her military power has been tested and generally recognized. Her chances of success in her program for reconstruction are better than many foreign observers are willing to grant. These circumstances have thrown everything off balance in the power structure of the Far East.

In reappraising the problem of China and of the Far East, it is useful to recognize first of all that the new China led by the Communist government in Peking is here to stay. There are no doubt many who would consider such an acceptance of reality as an act of plain defeatism. The truth of the matter is, however, that the maintenance of an anti-Communist attitude will not help change the course of events, for underlying the Communist seizure of power, there is the larger issue of the new China in the making. The greatness of the problems raised by the advent of this new China calls for much sounder measures of statesmanship and vision for their solution than those expressed in an emotional bias against Communism. In fact, the sooner the world faces this reality and devises measures to deal with it, the sooner will there be more stable relations among nations.

As we have noted in the preceding chapters, Communism has fastened a tight hold on the Chinese nation. But the triumph of Communism has not been an isolated victory. It has seized total power because it has been inextricably welded into the pulse of the Chinese Revolution. The time to forestall the triumph of Communism in China was in the early stages of the Revolution, under the Republic and during the Kuomintang period. Since the non-Communist groups then in power failed to offer adequate leadership to the Revolution, the mandate, so to speak, passed to the new group of Communist leaders, who, reading China's history with a greater insight than their predecessors, guided the Revolution to its climax. Now that the Revolution has achieved success, to treat the problem of China by a condemnation of its leadership is to miss the importance of the issue completely.

Clearly, powerful forces are at work which will make the coming age one of the greatest in Chinese history. Here, again, by greatness I do not imply a subjective judgment of approval, but a healthy development of national strength, coupled with the capacity to translate that strength into a successful rejuvenation. Among the developing internal trends which support the view that the new China is entering an age of greatness, the following are especially noteworthy. The Peking regime represents a strong central government, the like of which has not existed in China since the decline of the Manchu dynasty in the nineteenth century. The leadership of this strong government comes from a party possessed of great solidarity and iron discipline, and securely anchored in its command of all springs of national strength—political, military, economic, and social. In spite of skepticism from many quarters, its chosen course of socializing the nation's economy has been making great progress, progress that is destined to extend rather than reduce the measure of stability. The liquidation of the groups of privilege in the old social structure and the confiscation of their property have enriched the central treasury. For the first time within the memory of any living Chinese, Peking has translated into reality the phenomenon of a treasury with adequate resources to expend for the nation, a phenomenon that a modern Chinese could only read about with nostalgia in studying certain periods of history. The stupendous problem of governing a population of nearly six hundred millions has been effectively met by promoting the art of mass organization. As we have noted on numerous occasions, the entire Communist movement has adhered unswervingly to the policy of lessening the gap between the government and the people. The success of this policy alone, manifested in the tightness of control over all aspects of national life, will furnish the new regime with safeguards for the perpetuation of its power.

Then, too, the development of military strength and of nationalism is proceeding with full force. The broadening of the sociological background from which the armed forces are drawn has had the effect of mobilizing the entire manpower of the nation for the maintenance of a huge army. The stress on heavy and defense industries is designed to furnish a minimum of industrial and military matériel to sustain the fighting power of this great army. To be sure, the Chinese army will not be capable of large-scale offensive war in the near future, but it is doubtful whether it could be beaten by any invading force, barring a mass attack with nuclear weapons. Along with this defensive strength, one must take into consideration the potentialities of nationalism with reference to internal problems. Engaged in a fervent revival, the intense national pride of the people has stimulated them to emulate the achievements of those countries which humiliated China in the past. Peking's policy of fostering wide popular participation in all types of government activities, and of firing the enthusiasm of the young people in particular, aims precisely at guiding nationalism into useful channels of reconstruction. It is not altogether impossible that in the decades ahead China not only will tread a path similar to that of Japan following the Meiji Restoration but may attain an even greater strength in view of her enormous manpower and more abundant resources.

Finally, there seems to be no rival regime in sight which is capable of effectively challenging the power of Peking. The totalitarian government that has been imposed upon the people is not without its shortcomings. But, as I have said repeatedly, its greatest asset lies in the fact that it has brought peace and unification, and that it has helped to lift a great portion of the population out of starvation. Under such circumstances, for any rival group to argue for the destruction of the new regime merely on ideological grounds or on grounds of legitimacy is, to say the least, a purely academic pursuit. Unless a better economic and social program, not conceived in abstract and theoretical principles but proved to be of direct and tangible advantage to the masses, is offered to the people, it is certainly difficult to see any real threat to the existence of the new regime. Some day in the rather distant future, such an eventuality may conceivably take place. But at present and in the foreseeable future the Communist government is strongly in the saddle.

In view of these facts, it is clear that the Chinese Revolution under the Communist leadership represents an irresistible force, which cannot be stopped or checked. This mighty movement has aroused new hope in the Chinese people. For the first time in a hundred years China has succeeded in making the potential strength of her people felt in world affairs. This national resurgence must be respected, and not opposed. Thus to go along with the trend rather than against it is one of the primary conditions for the establishment of a new stable order in the Far East. It is the responsibility of the statesmen of all nations concerned to devise means within the given circumstances to find a way of living together, of minimizing the chances of war and strengthening the cause of peace.

One of the frequent oversights in the current quest for peace with China has been the failure to consider China's unique historical experience in foreign relations and the inability to appreciate the extent of the resultant difficulties. In her long history, China's relationship with the outside world has always been one of extremes. Until her encounter with the Western powers in the early nineteenth century, no nation of like magnitude existed in close proximity to China. Her external contacts were with the nomad tribes to the north and northwest. At that time, her power to assimilate the nomad invaders because of their lack of organizational skill and low cultural standard was her greatest weapon of defense and diplomacy. This contributed strongly to the insular character of Chinese culture. As a result, China became a world unto herself, conscious of the magnificence of her culture and disdainful of the outside world. Seeing no need for change or progress, she grew accustomed to interpreting her external relations in terms of the Empire above the "barbarians," of compassion from one and submission by the other, rather than coexistence on a basis of equality.

From this extreme of complacency, China was driven to the other extreme of humiliation following the advent of the Western powers in the nineteenth century. She found herself forced into a new and disconcerting relationship in which she was besieged and beaten by the industrial powers of the modern world. If the age-old complacency obviated the need to develop an understanding of normal international intercourse, the new onslaught of the West likewise made it hard for her to learn. Her successive stages of ignorance and resistance, imitation and frustration, reform and reaction, culminating in nationalism and revolution, only pointed to the truth that the country in its dire straits had no chance to gain a minimum of equilibrium which would enable her to order her foreign relations in the best interests of all concerned. Against this background, the new China is struggling to throw off the burden of both extremes of unfortunate experience and chart a course befitting her changed environment. What can be more natural than that the initial years of the new epoch should witness a frantic search for a formula that will help her guide her destiny?

There is no doubt that the United States and the Western powers should be prepared for major clashes of policy and interest with Communist China. Furthermore, such clashes are likely to be bitter and of fairly long duration.

The paramount consideration which must be accepted, however, is that a strong China is a force for peace. Throughout the years, there has been in certain quarters a fear of China's becoming strong. Such an attitude can only be considered inimical to the interests of world peace as well as to the interests of the Chinese people. A weak and disunited China has always been the breeding-ground of international rivalries. The best insurance for peace in Asia is a strong China. We have seen how unification has already enabled the Communists to effect a revolution in China's foreign relations. In spite of the many objectionable features the regime may have in other respects, the basic trend of the resurgence of China as Asia's leading power is a step in the right direction. For only through a strong China can there emerge a healthy power structure in the Far East.

The question, then, is not whether there should be a readjustment of relations in acknowledgment of China's new international status. The need for such a readjustment is beyond doubt, for the time is gone when the United States and the other Western powers were unopposed leaders in Asia. The real question is how the readjustment can be achieved, and whether it can be brought about peacefully.

Only yesterday, it seemed as though Communist China and the United States were perilously close to war. Two reasons accounted largely for this dangerous state of affairs. On the one hand, the United States was caught without a policy adequate to meet the new situation created by the sudden upsurge of Communist China. On the other, Communist China pursued a provocative policy, hoping thereby to assert China's big-power status by browbeating the United States, which she regarded as the stumbling-block in her path to greatness. More than anything else, the interplay of these two trends has been responsible for the alarming state of international relations.

The traditional policy of the United States toward China was to urge respect for China's independence and integrity, and observance of the principle of the Open Door by the interested foreign powers. This was a policy evolved against the background of its time, in which several elements were prominent. First, the imperialist powers—Britain, Japan, France, Germany, and Russia—constituted the dominant force on China's international scene at that time. Second, the United States, enjoying great economic prosperity and with much smaller military and trade involvements in the Far East, cared relatively little whether or not she commanded a major influence in Asia. Third, there had all along been the assumption that China's semi-colonial status would continue for a long time and consequently she should be given international assistance to build up her independence. Hence the United States spoke with idealism, and admonished the European powers to respect China's independence and integrity and the Open Door.

But now, within less than a decade, everything has changed so completely that none of these considerations is valid. The imperialist powers are gone. China has become strong and independent by her own means. The United States is no longer a semi-detached member in the concert of foreign powers. She is deeply involved in the new alignment of powers, with no one but herself holding the front line against the militant nationalism of Communist China. The basic predicament of the United States is that her traditional concepts regarding China are no longer applicable, while new ones have not yet been developed to meet the requirements of the new age.

Meantime, Communist China, intoxicated with her triumphant rise to power and strengthened by her alliance with Soviet Russia, has pursued her course of intense hostility to the United States as a means of winning recognition, and, to make matters worse, it seemed for a time that such a strategy would actually bring victory to Peking. Alarmed by the turn of events, a number of the allies of the United States as well as of the Asian nations clamored loud for the relaxing of tension. The sincerity of these nations in seeking to avert the danger of war, of course, was not to be doubted. But the effect of their appeal, which curiously enough was directed to the United States rather than to both sides, was a further deterioration of the international situation. Not realizing that the so-called tension was a symptom rather than the root cause of the disharmony, they would have the United States go along muddling through one dilemma and then another with dubious palliatives—a situation so aptly described in the Chinese saying: *"t'ou t'ung yi t'ou, chiao t'ung yi chiao"* ("rushing to nurse the head when the head aches, and rushing to nurse the foot when the foot aches"). The years from the end of the Korean war to the Bandung Conference will perhaps go down in history as marking a period when the peace in the Far East was taxed to the utmost.

Fortunately, since Bandung there has been a definite improvement in the situation. It has become increasingly clear that the inevitable readjustment in international relations need not be through war but can be achieved by peaceful means. It is of course too early to know whether the United States has evolved a new policy to fill the former vacuum. Nor can one say with certainty that Communist China has renounced her strategy of defiance of the United States in her battle for great-power status. But the direct talks between the two sides are a fact. No matter how fast or slow the progress of these talks may be in tackling the issues existing between the two countries, it is none the less clear that Peking and Washington share a common desire to break the deadlock between them. There is bound to be a period of probing and mutual testing of position. It is quite conceivable that the period of "no war, no peace" may stretch over a considerable length of time. But probing and testing are preludes to understanding, and the outcome is bound to carry the world farther away from war and closer to peace.

Let us examine briefly the reasons why, despite all the obvious tension, it is almost inevitable for Communist China and the United States to come to an ultimate readjustment of their differences. The first and foremost factor is that the aggressive expansionism of Communist China has effectively been checked by the United States. Of course, from a long-range standpoint, the United States has not yet entirely evolved a new Far Eastern policy. But the concrete measures taken during the Truman and Eisenhower administrations have been both sound and constructive. The fast and farsighted decision of President Truman to carry out the military sanctions of the United Nations in Korea in 1950 and the resolute action of President Eisenhower in 1955 to obtain the Congressional resolution for the defense of Formosa have been powerful factors in curbing Peking's aggression and in initiating a gradual build-up of a more stable order in the Far East.

As a result, the maximum gain the Communists can expect is a further extension of the power of the Vietminh in Indo-China. Aside from that, Peking's military advance in other areas has been arrested. Such a standstill cannot but affect Peking profoundly, because time is important for her. If her expansionism cannot win quickly, it will not win at all.

Thus it may be said that Peking has been forced to retreat to a more cautious policy. It now appears too risky to direct new aggressive attacks against the United States. Rather than look for new gains, Peking has grown anxious to conserve whatever power she has already won. Such a turn, it must be emphasized, is a great contribution to the cause of peace in general. For China, it has curtailed her vainglorious dreams of foreign conquest and compelled her to turn her energies to internal reconstruction, which she so sorely needs. As for the rest of the world, the chances of war are fewer now than they would have been had the United States not stepped into Korea and the Formosa Strait.

Along with the curbing of Chinese aggression, the operation of the Sino-Soviet Alliance has hit a snag. The offensive inspired by the alliance in 1950 was based on three assumptions. First, it was taken for granted that the United States would not resist the offensive with force. Second, immense gains were expected in view of the unpreparedness of the United States and the Western nations in general. Third, in the scheme of things as it looked in 1950, China was to act in complete concert with Russia, with every move representing a part of a joint Sino-Soviet strategy. None of these assumptions has come to pass. It took Peking and Moscow little time to discover that the

United States was not only prepared but determined to act. Then, too, since the first part of the plan misfired, the rest has continually been moving contrary to schedule. In the face of repeated affirmations by the United States of her determination to defend Formosa, Peking's demand that Formosa be "liberated" has brought increasing embarrassment to Moscow and has exposed the doubtful aspects of their alliance. It was Soviet Russia's policy to stir up Chinese bellicosity to a certain point, for this would serve Russia's political aims in Europe, weaken Anglo-American relations, and tie down American forces in the Far East. But as Chinese ventures moved perilously to the brink of a major war that might lead Peking to invoke the mutual-assistance clauses of the alliance, Moscow's inclination has been to restrain the action of Peking and to avoid a showdown with the United States. Reports have already been heard about the great strain China is imposing on Soviet economy.

Furthermore, China has been expanding her own strength and building up her own sphere of influence, in a manner quite different from the original conception of a joint Sino-Soviet strategy, if not opposite to it. From what has been said in the preceding chapters, several salient trends are noteworthy. The utilization by Peking of the fighting in Korea and of the prolonged truce talks to increase her military power is too important a development to ignore. It is as a result of this curious aspect of events that Communist China has grown to be such a strong military power. Then, the fact that China bore the entire brunt of the fighting in Korea has resulted in the creation of a paramount position for her rather than for Russia in the affairs of Korea. One must not discount the possibility that, in the long view, China's action in Korea was designed to forestall Russian domination. As for the developments in Indo-China, they seem to point to the same end. The victory of the Vietminh was primarily due to Chinese help. Observers at Geneva might have been impressed by the duet staged by Molotov and Chou as spokesmen for the Vietminh, but it was Chou who spoke the broker's word to Mendès-France which clinched the˙deal.

More recently Peking's extended campaign to woo the Asian nations is of even greater significance. In this quest for Asian unity, the appeal of China as a model of national rejuvenation has far surpassed any inducement Moscow may have to offer. Even if Peking's effort in this direction were not to meet with great success, she is destined in any case to have an increasing voice among Asian nations, and Soviet Russia must of necessity yield that leadership to her. All these trends may be assumed to indicate that in the short period of three or four years, China has actually been traveling away from the original spirit of the alliance. What was initially intended as a joint Sino-Soviet offensive against the West has now become China's own build-up of her regional security and leadership. This gradual reorientation of Peking's policy, leading away from the alliance toward greater independence of action, will not fail to contribute its share in the making of the new order in the Far East.

So far we have considered only the political undercurrents in the international ferment in the Far East. But the economic forces are no less significant. It is true that China has been making progress in her reconstruction with whatever aid she has received from Soviet Russia. But for large-scale industrial expansion she needs a greater amount of capital than can be managed from her own resources or obtained from Russia. Her only recourse for assistance on such a scale will be to look to the West, particularly to the United States. The United Nations embargo, moreover, has had an adverse effect on China's economy. With the bulk of her foreign trade limited to Russia and her east European satellites, China cannot experience full economic growth. In trade, too, she needs the West. Thus far China has been tightening her belt to ensure a good start with her industrialization. But for sustained and full-fledged development, she will be constrained to look for new sources of assistance.

Reference has been made to Peking's campaign to win Asian friends for herself, apart from the alliance with Russia. There are other directions in which this campaign will affect the emerging international order. China may alarm the countries on her immediate border, such as Thailand and Cambodia, with her great military power. But for the most part, she has to live among the great group of Asian nations as one of them. Not only does the very size of Asia make it impossible for her to duplicate the behavior of Russia in eastern Europe, but the nations of Asia are already wary of China's ambitions. This was amply shown at the Bandung Conference, as we have noted previously. Furthermore, the bid for Asian leadership will not go unchallenged. It will encounter the keen competition of the United States. SEATO has offered one rallying-point for nations interested in setting up a bulwark against the spread of Chinese Communism. The economic aid program of the United States has made a beginning in building up the internal strength of the Asian nations. The situation thus hangs in the balance, as far as the capacity of China to aid the Asian nations is concerned. True, these Asian nations are opposed to the imperialism of the white man, an issue that Peking can exploit to her advantage. But they are no less opposed to the imperialism represented by Communist China, a situation that she must endeavor to overcome if she is to earn the place of their friend and leader. Thus developments in this direction warrant the conclusion that, if Peking succeeds at all in building up an Asian bloc under her own leadership, that bloc will of necessity be a counterweight both to Soviet Communism on the one hand and to Western democracy on the other. Mao Tse-tung, who avows that one must lean either to imperialism or to socialism may yet find, in his bid for Asian leadership, that after all a third road does exist.

On account of these powerful undercurrents, the direct negotiations between China and the United States will ultimately lead to a new order in the Far East. As I have said, there will be long months of probing and testing. There may be stretches of smooth sailing. There may be halts and crises. But one thing is certain: these undercurrents in themselves cannot lead to a solution; they need direction if the long-sought end is to be brought to fruition. Herein lies the greatest challenge to the leaders of all parties concerned.

It is of course impossible to prescribe specific measures for our future endeavor. But the broad principles governing such an endeavor would presuppose a twofold direction: a positive respect for China as the great power in Asia, and effective steps against the world-revolutionary aspects of Chinese Communism.

There are many ways of expressing respect for China's

new position. But the first approach on the part of the Western powers should be to afford China the opportunity to work out her own destiny. This does not only mean noninterference in the narrow sense, but tolerance and understanding on a broad scale so that the prejudices and bigotry which hamper a creative spirit of co-operation among nations can be overcome. The conditions of the Chinese society and economy are so vastly different from those of the Western nations that to try to alter the inevitable trend of China's evolution is simply out of the question. The very fact that the Communist movement has succeeded in China is enough to make one ponder over this point. The living-standards of the masses are so low and such a large section of the Chinese people have been without any private property that socialization of the nation's economy cannot be expected to impose much hardship on the majority of the population. This is perhaps the main reason why the Communist regime can succeed in its program. Further, the co-operative method of production and consumption has always been strong in the Chinese family system. When this system was broken by the war, its members killed or scattered throughout the country, a natural opportunity was created for the Communists to step into the vacuum and build again on the old basis of a co-operative economy. Communism thus does not strike the Chinese as so sharp a break with their past mode of living as it might another people.

The Communist government has many features that are opposed and even repugnant to the democracies of the West. This, however, does not alter the fact that the Communist government has piloted the Chinese Revolution and is in effective control of the country. If the West were to attempt further to hinder this process, China's reaction could only be to resist such foreign pressure to the utmost. Progress should rather be sought through a due recognition of her strength and by encouraging her to develop her national poise and equilibrium.

Despite what has been said above regarding the gradual orientation of Peking away from her alliance with Soviet Russia, it may be taken for granted that China's ties with Soviet Russia will not easily be relinquished. The alliance of 1950 is a great adjunct of the big-power front that China presents to the world. Rather than move directly for the abandonment of this relationship, it would be the better part of wisdom to let the alliance weaken by itself. Aside from the political front, which adds to Peking's advantage, it is doubtful whether the operation of the alliance can satisfy the needs of Peking. For unless Russia can persuade the West to disarm, an outcome that is extremely improbable, she will not be able to supply China with the necessary military and economic aid.

This leads us to a second approach in expressing respect for China's new position as the great power in Asia. Russia's inability to furnish sufficient aid to meet Peking's needs creates the opportunity for the West to drive a wedge between the two Communist partners. By opening up trade and extending economic aid to China, for instance, the United States may find the most useful means of winning China away from Soviet Russia. China's greatest present need is to be enabled to expand her internal strength on the basis of what she has thus far achieved. The countries that help in her internal development will allay Chinese suspicions and will be looked upon as friendly. The key to undermining the Sino-Soviet Alliance thus is not direct pressure but rather the indirect method of economic assistance.

In this connection it must be stated that the West's anti-Communist policies and Peking's close ties to Moscow have been interlocked in a vicious circle of cause and effect. Trade embargoes, for instance, were instituted at first as a punitive measure against Peking's aggressive campaign. But as a result of the embargoes, Peking was driven even closer to Moscow. The continued maintenance of such trade barriers thus becomes a matter of doubtful virtue. The idea that Peking will hold inflexibly to her alliance with Russia must be considered somewhat naïve. On the whole, one nation functions pretty much like another, whether it is communistic or capitalistic. It moves in whichever direction serves its best interests. If the United States were to open up trade with China, the pro-Soviet slant of the Chinese economy would almost certainly fall off. If extensive aid were sent, even China's drive toward socialism might take on an aspect of moderation. There is no hard and fast position as a result of which Peking can not enter into amicable relations with the United States or with any other nation in the West. Soviet Russia herself is a case in point. Even to a greater degree than China, Soviet Russia represents a serious menace to the West. Yet she maintains regular relations with the United States and the nations of western Europe. Although a Communist power is ideologically hostile to the capitalistic nations of the world, this need not prevent it from entering into extensive relations with them. If the United States were to carry out a policy that would substantially contribute to the development of the internal power of Communist China and her role of leadership in Asia, it may be taken for granted that China's policies, both domestic and foreign, would undergo important changes.

But no measure of understanding and no amount of trade or economic aid can fully satisfy Communist China's aspirations until open recognition is made of her new international status. This is perhaps the most important factor whereby the West can contribute to the achievement of stability in Asia. So long as the Communist regime is the *de facto* government of the country, and so long as its authority is not effectively challenged by a rival government, formal diplomatic recognition and membership in the United Nations should be accorded her at an appropriate time. Such formal acknowledgment of China's status will hardly boost China's position, because a nation can scarcely be lifted to any station greater than that obtained by virtue of her own strength. But it will substantially help the cause of peace. Recognition of China's sovereignty and legitimate aspirations will further the success of the anti-aggression stand of the West. It will deprive Peking of any justification for its accusations. It will lead Moscow to hesitate before inciting Peking to fresh provocative acts. It will bring the allies closer to one another. Above all, it will allay the fears of the surrounding Asian nations. As a *rapprochement* between Communist China and the West draws near, this respect for China's new position will inject life into their new relationship. Otherwise, China will not be able to balance herself between Russia on the one hand and the United States on the other.

The establishment of Communist China as a strong Asiatic power, of course, will not suffice unless it is accompanied by an ability to maintain a full measure of independence. For only independence can prevent foreign domination and sustain a nation's self-balance. The conscientious objectors to granting Communist China recognition and admission into the United Nations are apprehensive lest she become a willing tool of Soviet Russia. It would be well, however, to give thought to another aspect of that question. If respect were accorded China's new position and strength, would it not in turn help heighten her spirit of independence? We must not forget the great historical fact that the Chinese Communists built up their power without outside help. Such a regime, having risen in its own right, will by its very nature refuse to be dwarfed by subservience to Moscow. The new China has an independence of will which one does not find in Russia's east European satellites. This is the chief reason why those satellites have thus far failed to develop into a positive force for the reconstruction of Europe. China, on the other hand, is no handmaid of Russia. She stands on her own feet and is both willing and able to order her own affairs. It is significant that the attempts of pro-Soviet elements to usurp power in the Chinese Communist Party from its early days to the present have been defeated swiftly and easily. Even Russia herself appears to recognize the futility of attempting to control Mao Tse-tung and his associates.

I have said in a preceding chapter that one of the motives which prompted China to align herself with Soviet Russia was fear occasioned by their geographical proximity. While such geopolitical factors are still valid, it is precisely the same psychology that originally led to the conclusion of the alliance that now constitutes its basic weakness. Like any other creation of fear, the Sino-Soviet Alliance cannot indefinitely prosper on such a relationship for the simple reason that fear either leads to dissolution or dissipates itself. In the case of Communist China, her fear of Soviet Russia has been wearing thin, noticeably during the last few years. The fact is that the spirit of independence is for the Chinese Communists a necessary condition for their own survival. There will be frequent shifts on the part of the Communist leaders from "orthodoxy" to "deviation" and vice versa, but the central fact is that they will have to move in harmony with Chinese conditions if they are to stay in power.

Certainly it is most unrealistic to assume that the Communist regime in China will of necessity run a course indistinguishable from that pursued by Russia. It is true that Communist rule has turned both Russia and China into great world powers. But closer examination will reveal a world of difference between them. Russia has become a great power with an industrial strength which approaches that of the United States. China, on the other hand, still has her center of gravity in agriculture. With a population three times that of Russia and four times that of the United States, and with three quarters of that total engaged in agriculture, China is strong in manpower but far behind any other great power in industrial and military potential. If the targets of her Five-Year Plan were fulfilled in 1957, China's production of steel would be only 4,000,000 metric tons, as against the 120,000,000 tons of the United States; of coal, 113,000,000 tons as against 453,000,000; and of electricity, 16,000,000 kilowatt-hours as against 442,000,000. Such an nation can be invincible in defense, but certainly will be incapable of major aggression.

Even within China's own borders, it is extremely doubtful whether the Communist rule will bring results like those observed in Russia or any other totalitarian state. It seems altogether too precipitate to believe that the Chinese Communists will be able to wipe out every vestige of the past and its hold upon the Chinese people. The four thousand years of Chinese history were characterized by absolute monarchy and by the predominance of privilege. But tyranny overshadowing the lives of the masses was not part of the process. On the other hand, Russian history is the very epitome of tyranny, and German history, of iron control. The Bolshevik and Nazi regimes ran true to the nature of these past trends in their respective countries. Is it then beyond reason to believe that the weight of four thousand years of experience, with the accent of the entire national spirit on moderation and humanism, will leave some imprint on the direction that the new China takes?

Contemporary accounts of the far-reaching effectiveness of Communist indoctrination and thought-control must be accepted with some reservation. After all, the Chinese are not without experience in this connection. The distance between the brain-washing of the present and that imposed by the Manchus in the seventeenth century is not so great as might be supposed. The early years of Manchu rule witnessed one "blood bath" after another as the ruling dynasty tried to stamp out all dissident thinking and demanded the unconditional submission of the people. On the surface, the Manchus had their way, especially with the young. Yet a subtle loyalty to the old way of life was passed on from generation to generation and the Manchus never succeeded in forcing the people from their accustomed grooves. An important point to bear in mind is that the

Chinese people are highly rationalistic and agnostic, and do not lend themselves readily to evangelical conversion. Their age-old saying *"Ku wang t'ing chih"* ("Just pretend to listen"), which counsels hearing the other person but holding on to one's own beliefs, can hardly have grown suddenly meaningless. The Communist regime may push its indoctrination or brain-washing to the utmost. But unless the very nature of the Chinese people has undergone a mysterious change, such efforts cannot be entirely successful. Long ago, Kublai Khan found that fighting the Chinese was like thrusting a hand into a feather cushion. On the surface, there appeared to be no resistance, but the cushion never failed to return to its original shape. Thus, to depict the current Chinese scene as a reproduction of events in Russia is to ignore the Chinese temperament completely. The Communists are still in the process of evolving their institutions. As time passes, we may expect these to take on some semblance of China's age-old historical pattern rather than that of other lands.

If the establishment of China's leading position in Asia and the development of a spirit of independence in her national policy are the first prerequisites for a new order in the Far East, a necessary second prerequisite is the adoption of effective steps against the world-revolutionary aspects of Chinese Communism. In other words, while China should be accorded recognition of her new position and strength and left free to work out her own destiny within her own borders, she must be brought to abandon her policy of unbridled expansion. Since the rise of the Communists to power, they have on numerous occasions declared that their government would not content itself with the overthrow of imperialism in China but would continue to wage war against world imperialism until the latter is destroyed. This design of world revolution is the worst enemy to peace in Asia, and far more sinister than Japan's ambition to conquer continental Asia prior to World War II. If such a policy were allowed to develop, the point at which words give way to deeds would some day be reached and all hope of a new Asiatic order would come to an end.

It is therefore of the utmost importance that the talks between Communist China and the United States should not be viewed as a cure-all. To use them as feelers leading to a well-affected *rapprochement* between China and the West represents but one important endeavor. No less important is the parallel task of providing safeguards against the new regime's dogma of world revolution. Fortunately, there are great odds against the realization of such an ambition. It should be recalled that the Soviet regime in Russia in the initial years of its existence also advocated such a program, but soon abandoned it in favor of the policy of "one-state socialism." In all probability, this is the road that Communist China will have to pursue in the years ahead.

None the less, it is useful to take stock of what can be done in this direction. As has been said repeatedly, the determination and preparedness of the United States to resist Peking's aggression has already compelled China to set aside her plans of conquest in certain peripheral areas and to turn her attention to the tasks of internal reconstruction. The sustained effort of the United States to stop aggression wherever it occurs is perhaps the paramount need of the day. In all likelihood, Peking has come to the conclusion that she is not equal to a contest of strength with the Western world. But unless full preparedness is maintained at all times, there is no assurance that her ambition will permanently be contained.

China's latest effort appears to be bent on extending her influence over the Asian nations. The major factor in her favor is a similarity in the historical background of most of the Asian nations, in the colonial or sub-colonial status from which they are now emancipating themselves. There are differences, however, which weigh heavily against too close an affiliation and against the exclusion of the West. For one thing, the economic and social conditions of most of these nations are not identical with those which existed in China. There is not the same population pressure on the land. There is poverty, but famine and drought are not the ever-present specters that they have been in China. It is therefore not likely that the Asian nations can be aroused to support a revolution modeled on the pattern of the Communist Revolution in China. Moreover, many Asian leaders, well steeped in the democratic philosophies of the West, not only are opposed to the Communist system but have the moral and material strength to carry out that opposition. Still further, most of these Asian nations have already benefited considerably from the Point Four Program, United Nations technical assistance, the military and economic aid of the United States, and the Colombo Plan for Co-operative Economic Development in South and Southeast Asia. If this aid can be brought into line with the essential needs of the Asiatic peoples living in the milliards of villages, Communist China even with Moscow's backing will have to go a long way before she can exceed or even match it.

Moreover, in spite of Chou En-lai's assurances that "revolution cannot be exported," and in spite of the fact that Peking has begun to make some overtures by abandoning her policy of claiming the allegiance of overseas Chinese, the possibility of Communist subversion in the various Asian nations has by no means passed. The famous five principles advocated by Peking (respect for sovereignty and integrity, nonaggression, noninterference, equality and mutual benefit, and peaceful coexistence) are so broad and so subject to varied interpretation that the Asiatic countries do not see in them adequate safeguards against Communist infiltration and subversion. No less a staunch friend of Communist China than Nehru himself has said: "Most of these countries are afraid, not of what governments do officially, but of what they might do *sub rosa* through the activities of the Communist parties in these countries. . . . If there were such a thing as a nationalist Communist party, a party which had nothing to do with another country, that would be a different matter. . . . The difficulty comes in because that party in your country is . . . intellectually, mentally, and otherwise tied up with other groups in other countries. And the other country might well utilize that for its own advantage." These are some of the aspects of the problems which the leaders of the West as well as of Asia should thoroughly explore in order to devise measures to defeat whatever infiltration or subversion may be attempted by Peking.

In addition to the steps suggested above, the defensive system of SEATO, representing as it does the massive power of the West coupled with the military aid given to such nations as Pakistan, Thailand, and the Philippines, is of considerable importance. In the last analysis, it was the effect of this system that in the winter of 1954–5 compelled

Peking to re-think her strategy of defiance and ultimately to turn to the policy of seeking direct talks with the United States. Equally important is the establishment of a policy that could offer greater hope and instill greater confidence in the Asian nations than the five principles held forth by the Communists. Such a policy, to achieve its purpose, must strive to strengthen the governments in the Asian countries, hasten their economic reconstruction, raise the standard of living of their peoples, and promote bonds of cooperation among them so that their strength to resist Communist infiltration can be increased. The ultimate objective of such a policy is not to draw the Asian nations to the Western side of the cold war, but rather to build them into a strong and independent regional group capable of steering itself in defense of its own interests.

Finally, the old concept of "Europe First, Asia Last" must be abandoned by the nations of the West. If this outmoded notion is allowed to persist, it can do infinite harm to the Far East. For by underrating the importance of Asia the Western leaders may unconsciously give scope to the expansionist tendencies of Peking. It is not too much to say that some of the existing tension has been indirectly caused by the undertones of appeasement inspired by this school of thinking. If China's nationalism is to be made a constructive rather than a destructive force, every one of the interested nations in Europe and America not only must defend its position against Peking's threat but must adopt a new conviction that what is not good for Asia cannot be good for Europe.

It is idle to think that peace will come soon in the Far East. But it is my belief that a major world war growing out of the tension between China and the West is extremely unlikely. Peking is basically unequal to a show-down with her chosen adversary. In spite of all her tough talk, she must refrain from the desperate plunge. To be sure, she might venture minor risks in order to revive and utilize tension. But, by and large, Peking would hardly dare carry out a major breach of the peace, for the simple reason that its consequences would be suicidal for herself.

As the direct talks between China and the United States develop, the clear intent to avoid force or the threat of force will emerge as the required condition for continued negotiation. On this basis, one step will follow another in exploring a settlement of the broader issues. In the great tasks which lie ahead, one can hardly overstress the importance of strengthening both the forces leading to an acceptance of China's new position and those leading to the defeat of her world-revolutionary ambitions. Unless one accompanies the other, bargaining on piecemeal issues will consume an inordinate amount of time and may not lead to any lasting settlement. Only when China is prepared to abandon her aggressive expansionism in any form and when the West accords her full acknowledgment of her new strength and position can negotiation on specific issues take on real significance. When that stage is reached, then such questions as the recognition of the Communist regime and its admission into the United Nations will be ready for consideration. That will be the day when membership in the United Nations will be meaningful and when Peking will fit into the international organization and will be ready to serve as a positive force for world peace.

There remains the question of the future evolution of the Sino-Soviet Alliance. With the growth of the forces poised against the spirit of the alliance, the question arises: will the alliance be completely reversed and will the end be war between China and Russia? In answering, it must be made clear that the forces opposing the Sino-Soviet Alliance, as discussed above, seek only to defeat the aggressive aspects of that partnership and not to set China and Russia against each other as enemies. Close ties between China and Russia for peacetime co-operation can still be of great significance. There is therefore strong reason to believe that the weakening of the Sino-Soviet Alliance will result not in war but in a new set of relationships between the two countries. Of course, Russia may be expected to try at every possible opportunity to encourage Chinese expansionism in order to push back the rival powers without risking a major world war. But she undoubtedly knows better than anyone else that there is a limit to this process and that the limit is already near at hand. Once that limit is reached, Russia's tactics will themselves undergo a change. They will then carry her along with China's new international environment and, through China's role as a leading power in Asia, help create a new international balance, with power divided and distributed among China, Russia, Japan, and the United States. Russia's greatest apprehension in the Far East is a strong Japan. So long as China can serve as a counterweight against the resurgence of a militaristic Japan or the combination of Japan and the United States, Russia's interests will have been secured.

In any consideration of the future of Sino-Soviet relations, the growth of China's internal strength is a factor to be kept constantly in view. In 1949 China was not yet on her own feet. Consequently, she could not afford to antag-

onize Russia. But if we project our view to 1957 or 1962
(target dates for the completion of her reconstruction
plans), China's progress should put her in quite a different
position. She cannot expect to be as strong as Russia, but
neither will she be weak. In the past it was China's utter
weakness that offered continuous temptation to Russian
encroachment. From the invasion of the Amur region
in the mid-nineteenth century, through the capture of
Kuldja, Port Arthur, and Dairen, and the deep inroads
made in Manchuria, Mongolia, and Sinkiang, Russia's
predatory acts followed a rapid crescendo in direct proportion to the worsening of China's plight. But whenever
China showed signs of recovery and strength, Russia retreated. For, above all, Russia understands power and fears
it. The increase in the strength of the Chinese Communist regime should supply a stabilizing factor hitherto
nonexistent between the two countries. The recent Soviet
overtures to Tito of Yugoslavia afford an instructive lesson.
So long as China does not become a threat to Russia—and
it is quite clear that in the foreseeable future China cannot possibly outstrip Russia in industrial and military potential—Russia will gain a new respect for this great
neighbor and will explore new avenues of co-operation
with her. When two giants meet, they do not come to blows
easily, because they know that the outcome will be ruin for
both.

Viewed in this light, the gaining of a spirit of independence by China is not at all incompatible with the maintenance of amicable relations between the two countries. On
the contrary, if the internal and external policies of Peking continue to unfold in the manner discussed above,
they may well put the relations between China and Russia

on a basis of normal rather than abnormal association. I have said before that geography has made China and Russia close neighbors, with a border longer than that linking any other two countries in the world. Historically, the type of relationship that China and Russia bear to each other is very old. Unwillingness on the part of either country to explore every possible avenue of friendly association is to create conditions against the interests of peace. The failure of the Kuomintang government to use positive efforts to establish good relations with Moscow, and its one-sided emphasis on the cultivation of Anglo-American friendship, must go down in history as a serious mistake. It is significant that Li Hung-chang in his day gave prior cognizance to the importance of Russia to China. Sun Yat-sen, too, championed and engineered the famous 1924 entente. This farsighted approach is being carried out once again by the Communist leaders in Peking. The question is not whether China should make friends with Russia: the necessity of such a policy is beyond doubt. The real question is how to make friends with Russia and how to make Chinese diplomacy succeed vis-à-vis Russia. Li Hung-chang failed completely to make it a success because China was then on the point of bankruptcy. Sun Yat-sen's entente also failed to achieve its objective, because China was in the initial stages of her national awakening and lacked both the spirit and the power to give the entente proper direction. Today China under the Communist regime can develop the necessary strength to deal with Russia as her equal. As a result, the ultimate fulfillment of a workable policy may be expected, in the not too distant future, to usher in that normal state of relationship which befits the two great powers on the Eurasian continent.

INDEX

Administrative Committees, 171
Administrative regions, 171
Agrarian reform, 49, 64
Agreement on Chinese Changchun Railway, Port Arthur and Dairen, 127, 136–7; *see also* Sino-Soviet Alliance
Agreement on Credits to China, 127; *see also* Sino-Soviet Alliance
Agriculture, socialization of, 173–88
Aid, *see* Soviet aid; United States: economic assistance
Airmen, *see* United States airmen
All-China Congress of the Soviets, First, 51
All-China Federation of Trade Unions, 92
Alliance, *see* Sino-Soviet Alliance
Alma Ata, 191
Amau declaration (1934), 134
Amur, 132, 230
Annam, 146
Anshan, 190
An-shih Revolt, 198
Anti-American campaign, 123, 125, 129, 139, 142
Asian hegemony, 126, 147–8, 156–7, 213–15, 225–6; *see also* Co-existence
Australia, 149
Autumn Harvest Insurrection, 51

Bandung Conference, 148, 159, 162, 209, 214
Belgium, 193
Beria, L., 92
Bill of Rights, 102
Blücher, General, 47

Bolsehevik revolution, 47, 81, 92, 168
Border areas, 31, 33, 52
Borodin, M., 47, 48
Bourgeois-democratic stage, *see* Chinese revolution
Boxer Protocol, 126
Boxer uprising, 16
"Brain-washing," 222
Burma, 148, 160
Burma Road, 193

Cadres, *see* Chinese Communist Party
Cambodia, 162, 214
Campaign against counterrevolutionaries (1951), 97, 170
Canada, 193
Canton, 18, 26, 47
Ceylon, 148, 160, 162
Chahar, 196
Chang-an, 198
Chang Fa-k'wei, 53
Chang Hsien-chung, 8
Chang-Kawagoe negotiations, 74
Chang Kuo-t'ao, 49, 55
Chekiang, 139, 141
Chen-feng movement, 97
Chen Tu-hsiu, 49, 55
Ch'en Yi, 52
Cheng Ho, 149
Chengchow, 191
Chiang Kai-shek, 25, 32–3, 36, 38–9, 74, 80, 89–90, 129, 136; *China's Destiny*, 194
Ch'ien Lung, 13
Ch'in dynasty, 4, 109
China: growth of spirit of independence, 219–22; new world position,

China (*continued*)
215–19; non-interference as respect for, 237–9; past experience in foreign relations, 205–6; recognition of new status, 219; traditional philosophy of government, 104

China's Destiny, see Chiang Kai-shek

Chinese Communist Party, 22, 86, 128; as political party, 97–8, 99; cadres, 58, 96–7, 102, 169, 176, 186, 187; correct line, 49; discipline, 96; *esprit de corps,* 53, 55; founding of, 54; membership, 96; organization of, 96–101; politburo, 90; Sixth National Congress, 51

Chinese Communists: and Chinese society, 216–17; anti-Communist campaigns, 39; ascendancy in Wuhan, 23; call for United Front, 36, 37; co-operation with Kuomintang, 21, 22; demand for coalition, 44; development since 1927, 28; early program, 23–4; guerrilla warfare, 41; ideology, 69; independent strength, 51; Liberated Areas, 44; persecution of, 54, 65; Russian advisers, 47; split with Kuomintang, 23; wartime expansion, 39; wartime policy, 40; *see also* Chinese Communist Party; Communist leadership; Kuomintang

Chinese revolution: bourgeois-democratic stage, 174; socialist stage, 174–5

Chinese Soviet Republic, 32, 51, 53

Ch'ing dynasty, 12, 66, 198

Ching T'ien, 4

Chingkanshan, 51

Chou dynasty, 4, 101

Chou En-lai, 51, 84, 101, 123, 127, 144, 149, 159, 161, 162, 185, 190, 213, 225

Chü Ch'iü-pai, 49, 55

Chu Hsi, 123

Chu Pei-teh, 68

Chu Teh, 39, 51, 52, 62, 84

Chün T'ien, 9, 77

Chungking, 39, 191, 194

Civil war (1947–9), 78

Classes, outlawed, 101

Coal, 168, 191, 192, 193

Co-existence, 157; five principles of, 148, 226

Cold war, 148, 161, 172, 195, 227

Collective farms, 179

Collectivization, 173, 179, 180, 187, 188, 197, 199; *see also* Socialization of agriculture

Colombo Plan, 225

Communist leadership: as practical rulers, 87–8; autocracy and dictatorship, 86–7; compared to Han leaders, 84; early differences, 28; future outlook, 92–3; stability of oligarchy, 90–2; training of leaders, 49; unified command, 55; *see also* Elite rule

Confucianism, 5, 85, 99, 105

Constitution of 1954, 102

Crusade against traditional culture, 113

Dairen, 230

Democracy: in underdeveloped countries, 29; negation of, 101–2, 103–4

"Democratic centralism," 101–2

"Democratic dictatorship," 101–2

Democratic League, 37, 68

Dien Bien Phu, 143

Dulles, J. F., 143

Dzungaria, 191

Eastern Tsin dynasty, 42

Economic regions, 11, 197–9

Eighth Route Army, 39

Eisenhower, Dwight, 210

Electric power, 191, 192–3
Elite rule, 85, 99–100; *see also* Communist leadership
Entente of 1924, *see* Sino-Soviet Entente of 1924
Extraterritoriality, 122

Family system, 7, 114–15
Fan Kwan, 84
Fang La Revolt, 8
Feudal system, 4, 7, 84, 99, 114
Finance, public, 167, 203
"Five-anti Movement," 97, 170
Five Dynasties, 134
Five-Year Plan, 167, 189–94, 199, 200, 221
Food, 168
Formosa, 136, 138, 139, 140, 152, 153, 155, 162, 164, 210, 212
France, 149
Fukien, 52, 139, 141, 154
Fu-pin, 66, 106
Fushun, 190

Geneva Conference (April–June 1954), 143, 147, 151, 213
Gentry, 79; *see also* Scholar-literati; Landlord-scholar class
Germany, 121
Grain collection, 183
Great Britain, 123, 129, 149, 153
Guerrilla diplomacy, 150, 163
Guerrilla warfare, 61, 67

Han dynasty, 4, 8, 66, 84, 85, 106, 125, 146
Ho Chi-minh, 146
Ho Lung, 51, 52
Ho-Umetsu Agreement, 74
Hongkong-Shameen Strike, 48
"*Hsiang-yung*," 80
Hsiao Ho, 84
Hsien-pi, 95, 196
Hsin dynasty, 9
Hsiung-nu, 95, 196

Huang Ch'ao uprising, 8
Hunan, 30, 56, 57, 74
Hung, Hsiu-chuan, 64
Hwai River Valley project, 194

Ideological Remolding Campaign, 115
Imperialist powers, 15, 82, 208
India, 131, 148, 153, 160, 193
Indo-China, 138, 211, 213
Indo-China War, 142–3, 145, 148
Indonesia, 148, 160, 162
Industrialization, program of, 188–200
Industries, nationalization of, 188–9
Inflation, 167
Intervention, absence of, 82
Iran, 160
Iraq, 160
Iron, 168, 191
Irrigation, 185

Japan, 16, 82, 127, 131, 138, 141, 145, 148, 152, 164, 192, 224, 229; war with, 36, 39, 45, 60, 77–8, 120
Juchen, 11, 95, 198
Juichin, 33, 52, 74

Kaifeng, 11, 198
Kansu, 196
Kao Kang, 92, 171
Khitan, 11, 95, 134, 196
Kiangsi, 30, 33, 52, 56, 68, 73, 74, 77
Korea, 138, 151; North Korea, 110, 138; South Korea, 140, 147
Korean armistice, 142
Korean War, 110, 124, 138–42, 144–5, 167, 172, 209, 212
Kotelawala, Sir John, 160
Kuan Yin, 84
Kublai Khan, 223
Kuldja, 230

Kuomintang, 98, 109, 231; and youth, 116–17; blockade of Shensi, 43; clash with Communists, 23; difficulties during war, 40, 41, 42, 77; failure of democracy under, 28, 34; leadership, 92; loss of gentry support, 79; Nanking government, 24; Nanking-Wuhan split, 23, 54; Northern expedition, 22, 120; peace talks with Communists, 45; reorganization of 1924, 18, 21, 73; revolution under Sun Yat-sen, 17; revolutionary program, 18–19, 20–1; tutelage, 26; Wang Ching-wei and left wing, 24; weaknesses, 27

Labor-exchange brigade, 176
Labor unions, 48
Lanchow-Tihwa line, 191
Land: Ching T'ien, 4; Chün T'ien, 9; concentration of holdings, 4, 9; confiscation of, 48; Kuomintang measures, 27, 33; land reforms, 9, 57, 174; nationalization of, 181, 183; population-land ratio, 10, 13; program of Sun Yat-sen, 19; reclamation of, 185; redistribution of, 30; rents, 27
Land Reform Law of 1950, 97, 169, 173
Landlord-scholar class, 85; *see also* Gentry; Scholar-literati
Landlords, 4, 5, 15, 17, 26, 57, 173, 174, 175, 182
Lenin, 183
Li Hung-chang, 231
Li Li-san, 49, 55, 56, 92
Li Tsu-ch'eng, 8
Liang-shan-pa, 65
Liaotung peninsula, 132
Lin Piao, 39, 52
Liu Pang, 84
Long March, 34, 55
Lukouchiao, 77

MacArthur, Gen. Douglas, 140
Machine works, 190, 191, 230
Malenkov, G., 92
"Manchukuo," 74
Manchuria, 130, 131, 133, 141, 179, 196, 198
Manchus, 12, 16, 222
Manila Pact, 49, 155
Mao Tse-tung, 29, 51, 52, 64, 66, 73, 84, 87, 89, 90–1, 101, 110, 123, 125, 126, 128, 134, 138, 187, 215, 220; as leader, 51, 53, 89, 91–2; Mao Tse-tung line, 30, 46, 69; place in history, 31; revolutionary thinking, 31, 32, 49, 50, 69; writings, 43, 44
Marshall, Gen. George, 45
Marxism-Leninism, 31, 69, 70, 72, 88, 188
Masses: base for government, 75; detachment of Kuomintang from, 7, 25, 26, 75; organization of, 7, 21, 30, 48, 56, 57, 58, 203
Matsu, 156
Maximum program, 174–5
Mendès-France, Pierre, 213
Metal works, 191
Military and Administrative Committees, 171
Military power, 105, 203; intervention in Korea, 110–11; methods for expanding, 107–11; militia, 107; outlook, 111; prior to 1949, 105–7; regular army, 107; Russian arms and advice, 111; since 1949, 107–8
Min-t'uan, 66
Ming dynasty, 8, 66, 144, 198
Minimum program, 174–5
Mohammedan revolts, 14
Molotov, V. M., 132, 133, 144, 155, 213
Mongolia, 230
Mongols, 196, 198
Mutual-aid team, 176–8, 187; long-

Mutual-aid team (*continued*)
term type, 177; short-term type, 176–7

Nanchang uprising, 51
Nanking government, 26; *see* Kuomintang: Nanking government
Nanking-Wuhan split, *see* Kuomintang: Nanking-Wuhan split
National Salvationists, 37, 68, 74
Nationalism, 118–25, 203–4
Nationalist government (Formosa), 154, 155
Nehru, J., 149, 160, 163, 226
New democracy, 69
New order in Far East, 205, 206–7, 215, 229
New Zealand, 149
Nien Fei rebellion, 8, 14
Ningtu uprising, 68
Northern Dynasties, 66, 106
Northern Expedition, *see* Kuomintang: Northern expedition
Northern Wei dynasty, 9
Nurhachi, 44

Oil, 191, 192, 193
On Coalition Government, 44; *see also* Mao Tse-tung
On New Democracy, 43; *see also* Mao Tse-tung
Open Door, 208
Overseas Chinese, 162

Pailingmiao, 190
Pakistan, 148, 149, 160, 162, 226
Pan-Asianism, 157–8
Paotou, 190, 197
Paotou-Lanchow line, 191
Peace and unification, 82, 83, 103, 186, 203, 204
Peasant associations, 57, 65
Peasant unions, 48
Peasants, 4; and Red Army, *see* Red Army; as revolutionary base, 29,

Peasants (*continued*)
30, 50, 56, 69; grievances under ancien regime, 6, 14, 27; peasant movement in Hunan, 50; peasant unions, 48; position under Communist government, 85, 86; possible measures against, 199–200; revolts in history, 8; under Land Reform Law of 1950, 169–70; under socialization of agriculture, 184–5
Peiyang generals, 17
P'eng Teh-huai, 39, 52, 84
People, Communist definition of, 63, 101
People's congresses, 101, 102
People's Livelihood, 19, 21, 32
People's militia, 44
People's Political Council, 44
Pescadores, 155
Philippines, 148, 149, 160, 226
Ping-hsing-kuan, 39
Pinghsiang, 191
Po Yi-po, 92
Point Four Program, 225
Political parties, 98
Population: growth, 10, 12, 13; mass migration of, 11; population-land ratio, 10, 13; population problem, 180, 185–6
Port Arthur, 133, 230
Price stabilization, 167
Privilege, groups of, 4, 5, 8, 15, 25, 29, 62, 71
Producers' co-operatives, 178–9, 186–7
Production, agricultural, 179, 183
Production, industrial, 83, 221
Proletariat, dictatorship of, 63, 70
Propaganda, 73

Quemoy, 156

Railways, 167, 191
Red Army, 33, 44, 51, 58, 64, 66, 79;

Red Army *(continued)*
as labor force, 60; changing composition of, 112; conscription law, 111; financing of, 68; genuine national army, 106; indoctrination of, 106; peasant base of, 30; *see also* Military power
Red Eyebrows, 8
Red River delta, 143
Reforms and revolution, 63–4
Regional governments, 171–2
Republic, 17, 18, 104–5, 109, 198
Revolts and rebellions, 8, 14, 64
Revolution (1911), 12, 17
Rhee, Syngman, 147
Romulo, Carlos P., 160
Rural environment, 59–62
Russo-Japanese War, 16, 145

San Min Chu I, 18, 19, 25, 28
Sang Hung-yang, 19
Scholar-literati, 5, 7; *see also* Gentry; Landlord-scholar class
SEATO, 148, 149, 155, 163, 214, 226
Secret societies, 97–8
Settlements, foreign, 122
"Seven Hates," 44
Sha-to, 95
Shanghai, 191
Shensi, 33, 198, 199
Shih Chin-t'ang, 134
Shimonoseki, Treaty of, 126
Shui Hu Chuan (All Men Are Brothers), 32, 65
Sian, 191
Sian incident, 38, 54
Sinification, reversal of, 94–6
Sinkiang, 130, 196, 230
Sino-Japanese War (1894–5), 16, 145
Sino-Soviet Alliance (1950), 110, 126, 158, 211–12, 217, 220–4, 228–31

Sino-Soviet Entente (1924), 21, 132, 231
Sino-Soviet relations: Chinese policy toward Russia, 230–1; future outlook, 228–31; Soviet policy toward China, 137, 212, 229; traditional Russian policy toward China, 131–3
Six States, 84
Socialist stage, *see* Chinese revolution
Socialization, *see* Agriculture, socialization of
Society, traditional, 4, 6, 24, 46, 94–5
Society under Communists, 85–6
Southern Sung dynasty, 42
Soviet aid, 133, 164, 194, 213
Soviet Russia, 18, 19, 21, 83, 122, 131, 142, 218, 221, 224; *see also* Sino-Soviet relations; Sino-Soviet Alliance
Sovietization, 94–6
Spheres of influence, 212–13
Stalin, 88, 138, 183
Steel, 168, 192, 193
Student Movement (1935), 74
Subversion, 226
Sui dynasty, 9, 109
Suiyuan, 196
Sun-Joffe Manifesto (1924), 126; *see also* Sino-Soviet Entente of 1924
Sun Lien-chung, 68
Sun Yat-sen, 17, 18, 20–1, 22, 24, 32, 56, 73, 89–90, 98, 100, 120, 122, 124, 128, 157, 231
Sung dynasty, 10, 11, 109, 198
Szechuan, 197

Tachen islands, 156
Taiping rebellion, 8, 14, 64, 80, 168
Taiyuan, 191

Talks, U.S.-China, *see* United States: bilateral talks with China

T'ang dynasty, 9, 66, 106, 125, 144, 199

T'ang Sheng-chih, 53

Tangku truce, 74

Tangut, 95

Tariff, 16, 122

Tarim Basin, 191

Tatung, 191

Taxation: Communist system of, 167, 170, 177, 184; pre-Communist period, 6, 10, 27

Tayeh, 191

Tension, 126, 147, 150, 153, 209

Textiles, 191

Thailand 148, 149, 160, 162, 214, 226

Thought control, 113

"Three-anti Movement," 97

Three-thirds system, 75

Tibet, 82

Tienshan range, 191

Tienshui-Chengtu-Kweiyang-Kunming line, 191

Tientsin, 191

Tihwa (Urumchi), 191

Tito, 230

T'o-ba, 95

Tonking, 146

Trade embargo, *see* United Nations: trade embargo

Transition to Socialism, 173, 182, 187

Treaty of Friendship, Alliance, and Mutual Assistance, 127, 133; *see also* Sino-Soviet Alliance

Triad Society, 98

Truman, Harry S., 140, 210

Tseng Kuo-fan, 15, 80

Tseng-yi Conference, 53

Tu-chüeh, 95, 193

T'un-t'ien, 66

Tung Chung-shu, 19

Tung Ling Party, 98

Turkey, 160

Turkistan, 132

U Nu, 149, 160

Unequal treaties, 15, 20, 26, 120, 122

Unification, 26, 81, 82, 83, 104, 118; *see also* Peace and unification

Union of Military Youth, 48

United Front, *see* Chinese Communists: call for United Front

United Nations, 124, 140, 143, 152, 155, 164; admission of Communist China, 164-5, 220, 228; sanctions, 210; technical assistance, 225; trade embargo, 164, 214, 218

United States, 83, 123, 126, 127, 128, 131, 137, 140, 149, 152; anti-American campaign, *see* Anti-American campaign; bilateral talks with China, 163, 210, 224, 227, 228; economic-aid program, 214; economic assistance, 214, 225; leadership in Asia, 214; Peking's hostility to, 209; present China policy, 207-8; resistance against aggression, 224-5; traditional China policy, 208; U.S.-Chiang Mutual Security Treaty, 163

United States airmen, 155, 156, 163

Uranium, 191

Versailles Conference, 120

Vietminh, 139, 143, 146, 147, 211, 213

Vietnam, 143, 146

Village, 5, 26

Village government, 27, 30, 57

"Volunteers," Chinese, 110

Wang An-shih, 19, 63, 64

Wang Ching-wei, 24, 48, 53, 134

Wang Mang, 9

Washington Conference, 120, 126
Water conservancy, 185
Wen Ti (Han dynasty) , 85
Western Hills group, 24
White Lotus uprising, 14
World revolution, steps against,
    223–7

Yang Yen, 10
Yangtze, 199

Yeh Chien-ying, 92
Yeh T'ing, 51
Yellow Turbans, 8
Yenan, 33, 34, 35, 77
Yenchang, 191
Youth, 115–16
Yuan (Mongol) dynasty, 12, 94
Yuan Shih-kai, 17
Yugoslavia, 230
Yumen, 191

DATE DUE